International Trade Regulation

The international trade regulatory system is a dynamic system that has been evolving throughout its history. Tension and conflict are part of the system. While calls for the abolition of the principal trade regulation authority, the WTO, have failed to understand this nature of the system, proponents for reforms have so far not paid sufficient attention to the evolving nature of tension and conflict. This book examines the evolving dynamics in international trade regulation from the conclusion of GATT in 1947 to the current crisis facing the WTO, from a perspective of emerging powers of developing countries with a focus of China as the latest force that demands reforms of the international trade regulatory regime.

There is an extensive body of scholarship on ideological struggles, the rise of developing countries, geopolitical contest, the emerging powers (especially China), the use, misuse or abuse of trading rules and so on. There is, however, a lack of a single concise research book that synthesises these underlying causes and factors into a coherent and precise analytical theme. This book attempts to fill this research gap by building upon the existing scholarship and placing the various tensions and conflicts in a perspective that treats them as dynamic factors that have propelled a continuing process of evolution of the international trade regulation.

The book will interest those researching on international trade regulation as well as development studies.

Zhiqiong June Wang is Associate Professor at the School of Law, Western Sydney University, Australia.

Jianfu Chen is Emeritus Professor at La Trobe University and Honorary Professorial Fellow at Melbourne University, Australia.

Routledge Research in International Economic Law

The Legality of Economic Activities in Occupied Territories
International, EU Law and Business and Human Rights Perspectives
Antoine Duval and Eva Kassoti

International Investment Protection within Europe
The EU's Assertion of Control
Julien Berger

Trade, Migration and Law
Free Movement of Persons in the South African Development Community
Victor Amadi

The Americanization of the World Trade Order
Asif H Qureshi

Reform and Regulation of Economic Institutions in Afghanistan
Haroun Rahimi

The Freest Market in the World
The Constitutional Logic of Economic Liberty in Hong Kong
Gonzalo Villalta Puig and Eric C Ip

International Trade Regulation
Evolving Dynamics and Shifting Foundations
Zhiqiong June Wang and Jianfu Chen

For more information about this series, please visit www.routledge.com/Routledge-Research-in-International-Economic-Law/book-series/INTECONLAW

International Trade Regulation

Evolving Dynamics and Shifting Foundations

Zhiqiong June Wang
Jianfu Chen

Routledge
Taylor & Francis Group
LONDON AND NEW YORK

First published 2023
by Routledge
4 Park Square, Milton Park, Abingdon, Oxon OX14 4RN

and by Routledge
605 Third Avenue, New York, NY 10158

Routledge is an imprint of the Taylor & Francis Group, an informa business

British Library Cataloguing-in-Publication Data
A catalogue record for this book is available from the British Library

ISBN: 978-1-032-23052-8 (hbk)
ISBN: 978-1-032-23064-1 (pbk)
ISBN: 978-1-003-27551-0 (ebk)

DOI: 10.4324/9781003275510

Typeset in Times New Roman
by Apex CoVantage, LLC

Contents

Preface and Acknowledgement

We are often told, by our social friends and, sometimes, by our students, that law is boring and, unfortunately, it is so for most people. Yet, law penetrates every aspect of our life as ground rules that we must comply with, as individuals, collectives or as nation states. Alternatively, we must suffer the consequences if we do not comply or if we break the rules. So, boring as it might be, we do need to understand the law and the consequences of non-compliance.

As academic lawyers with practice experiences in the early days of our career, it has always been clear to us that, if law is boring, it is more often than not caused by the very dry technical analyses that are offered to readers as explanations of law. Can we explain law to our readers without all the niceties of the dry technics? Or, more importantly, can we claim that we understand the law once we have acquired the knowledge of technical rules? Would it be a fundamental concern for us as educators that, among our many graduates there are always quite some who know so much yet understand so little about law?

Law in fact is a living force that exists and evolves in society and through time. It is boring only if we fully concentrate on technical details, important though they are. This is the same as in art or music or indeed any profession. Every art or music student will tell us how boring their profession might be if one has to undertake the meticulous study and routine practice of the technical details, and how much they envy us that we can simply appreciate paintings or enjoy music without the need to undertake the study of the boring bits. But, without a good knowledge of the technics in art or music, do we miss something that is important when we appreciate paintings or enjoy music? Or, instead, do we get more out of art and music if we actually understand the social context and technical skills of the time when the paintings or the music were produced?

In 2006, the British Broadcasting Corporation broadcast an eight-part series, entitled *Simon Schama's Power of Art*, on works of eight selected art masters. It was not an art history course, but it said much more than many works on art history. Each episode examined only a few works by the master selected for the episode. It focused on the context of the work and, most importantly, the transforming power of the works. Episode One, for example, was on *David with the Head of Goliath* by Caravaggio (Michelangelo Merisi Da). But we dare to say, the haunting image of *David with the Head of Goliath* is not what was left in the memory of the audiences; it is Caravaggio's transforming power that we remember – he used ordinary people's images to paint the high art that was then completely divorced from the great part of the society. Similarly, in Episode Two, one is impressed by the *Ecstasy of Saint Teresa* by Bernini (Gian Lorenzo), but the real impact is, once again, the transforming power of Bernini – he for the first time in art history added flesh and blood to marble sculpture and brought such sculpture to life. All eight episodes took a similar approach – focusing on context and the transforming power of the great masters; but none examined any of the technical details nor tried to encompass all great works of the masters.

The same can be said about how classical music is to be best appreciated. There are so many excellent analyses on technical innovation and unique features of the classical masters, and these certainly and greatly improve our understanding of the music. However, one could not stop thinking, very often, that, to the trained ear, would these analyses become distractions or even obstructions to the appreciation of the masterpieces, and to the untrained ear, what are the purposes of such analyses? More specifically, we all know that Beethoven's Seventh Symphony is the most performed among the master's nine symphonies and is said by the composer to be one of his best, but symphonies Five, Six and Nine perhaps are the most popular among the non-specialist audiences. And if we were to choose one of his nine symphonies as the one that best reflects the character of the master and his music, we probably would choose the Third and we probably would insist that, if one understands the Third, one understands Beethoven and his time.

The point is, can we understand a masterpiece without too much technical analysis? Or more precisely, is the context of a masterpiece only auxiliary to the understanding of the masterpieces or is it *the* clue to the understanding of the masters and their masterpieces?

Global trade regulation, principally represented by GATT/WTO, is a masterpiece. It is a complex and evolving structure and a body of mechanisms and principles that impact on the life of everyone. The technical analysis of the various aspects of it is critical and there are many excellent works on it, but the acquisition of this knowledge is only one way towards an understanding of the complex and complicated system.

'In law context is everything' (Lord Steyn), and context is about underlying currents, time and space. It is context that has often been neglected in many of these technical analyses, yet it is context that is indispensable in our understanding of the structure, mechanisms, principles and their actual functioning. This short research book, different from a large body of excellent literature on international economic order generally and GATT/WTO particularly, strives to reclaim the importance of context in the understanding of international economic order as reflected in international trade regulation. By close examination of the context, it offers a view that such an international economic order is meant to be an evolving one and its evolution is propelled by different forces at different times. With this in mind, it is argued that the global trade regulation system must respond to changing and changed geopolitical reality of a given time. And it inevitably will, judging by its own historical struggles since 1947 when the GATT was first agreed upon. In short, this is a book about the evolving dynamics that maintain as well as shift the foundation of international economic order.

This book is a result of academic endeavour of many years. It is also an enterprise of collaboration over an extended period of time. Importantly, it is a product of collaboration with equal contribution from each of us and we are therefore jointly responsible for the views expressed herein and any errors that might remain.

Undertaking such an enterprise cannot be successful without support from many people, including our students who have been the first audience to offer their honest views and opinions on our analysis. We have also presented some of our early works at conferences and seminars, and we are most appreciative of the comments made by colleagues on these occasions. We have also received generous support, assistance and friendship from many friends and colleagues in Australia, China and other countries, and we are most grateful to them all. We are particularly grateful to Dr. Elfriede Sangkuhl who assisted us in the final editing and proofreading of the manuscripts and who also made many thoughtful and helpful comments on the various chapters of the book.

June would like to express her deepest love for her beautiful and most adorable twins, Marcus and Matthew, whose love has opened her eyes to a new horizon in and perspective about life.

We also acknowledge that some materials contained in this book had earlier been published in journals and book chapters, but none was published in the current form and all of them have been further revised and updated.

Zhiqiong June Wang
School of Law
Western Sydney University
Sydney, Australia

Jianfu Chen
La Trobe University/
the University of Melbourne
Melbourne, Australia

Abbreviations

AB	Appellate Body (of the WTO)
ABC	Anyone-but-China
ACP	African, Caribbean and Pacific Countries
AIIB	Asian Infrastructure Investment Bank
ASEAN	The Association of Southeast Asian Nations
BRI	Belt and Road Initiative, alternatively, One Belt One Road
BRICS	Brazil, Russia, India, China and South Africa
ChAFTA	China – Australia Free Trade Agreement
CPTPP	The Comprehensive and Progressive Agreement for Trans-Pacific Partnership
DFAT	Department of Foreign Affairs and Trade
DSB	Dispute Settlement Body (of the WTO)
EAS	East Asia Summit
ECOSOC	Economic and Social Council
FANs	Friends of Antidumping Negotiations
FIPs	Five or the Quint
FTA	Free Trade Agreement
FTAAP	Free Trade Area of the Asia Pacific
G7	Group of Seven
GATS	General Agreement on Trade in Services
GATT	General Agreement on Tariffs and Trade
GDI	Global Development Initiative
GFC	Global financial crisis
GNP	Gross National Product
GSI	Global Security Initiative
GSP	Generalised System of Preference
IBRD	International Bank for Reconstruction and Development
IMF	International Monetary Fund
ITO	International Trade Organisation
IPEF	Indo-Pacific Economic Framework for Prosperity

LDCs	Least Developed Countries
MFN	Most-favoured Nation treatment
MOFCOM	Ministry of Commerce, People's Republic of China
NAFTA	North America Free Trade Agreement
NIEO	New International Economic Order
OMAs	Orderly marketing arrangements
PPA	Protocol of Provisional Application
PRC	People's Republic of China
PTA	Preferential Trade Agreement
RCEP	Regional Comprehensive Economic Partnership
RTAs	Regional Trade Agreements
S&D	Special and Differential Treatment
TiSA	Trade in Services Agreement
TPP	Trans-Pacific Partnership
TRIMS	Agreement on Trade-Related Investment Measures
TRIPS	Agreement on Trade-Related Aspects of Intellectual Property Rights
TTIP	Transatlantic Trade and Investment Partnership
UNCTAD	United Nations Conference on Trade and Development
UNDP	United Nations Development Program
USTR	US Trade Representative
VERs	Voluntary export restraints
WIPO	World Intellectual Property Organization
WTO	World Trade Organisation

Introduction

1. Three Struggles – Old and New in the Name of Pursuing Freer and Fairer Trade

The discussion of and debate on 'social issues' during the Uruguay Round (1986–93) of the GATT/WTO negotiations highlighted the potential impact of trade liberalisation on certain human rights. However, it would be wrong to assume that the link between trade liberalisation and human rights was only established in the late 1980s and early 1990s. In fact, these two issues were the twin considerations in the post-World War II reconstruction efforts and formed the cornerstone of the United Nations (UN).

However, trade liberalisation and the protection of human rights are based on two fundamentally different philosophical foundations – free market *vis* state intervention – at least in relation to economic and social rights, and other 'third generation' rights. Not surprisingly, the twin goals of trade liberalisation and human rights eventually parted company and each then took a rather different path and pace in development, as evidenced in the separate development of the UN and the GATT/WTO. The 're-union' of the two goals is a more recent development, but the union has hardly been a happy or harmonious one until this day. The struggle with this union is not so much a struggle between trade liberalisation *vis-à-vis* the protection of individual rights or specific collective rights such as labour standards and environment protection, as a struggle between trade liberalisation *vis-à-vis* the so-far ambiguous concept of the human right to development. While there has never been a clear definition of a human right to development, the struggle has been essentially fought in the name of global justice and equity, or in the language of trade, for a *fairer* trade system.

Meanwhile, there has always been a struggle within the trade regulatory system, a struggle for freer trade between nation states with less barriers to trade. Indeed, ever since the establishment of the GATT in 1947, the international trade regulatory system, principally consisting of rules

DOI: 10.4324/9781003275510-1

and mechanisms under the GATT/WTO, regional trade agreements and other inter-government cooperative agreements, has undergone continuing changes, mostly in the name and direction of trade liberalisation.

The previously mentioned two struggles (for fairer and freer trade) continue, with no end in sight. A new dimension to this struggle has emerged more recently, with its nature having become clearer with the rise of China. Thus arises a new struggle that is geopolitical in nature, initially fought in the form of regional agreements, but it has increasingly been reflected in demands for WTO reforms. Although it is geopolitical in nature, it is nevertheless fought in the name for a fairer trade order.

The history of international trade regulation is essentially a history of struggles for a freer and fairer regulatory system and, more recently, geopolitical domination. The system is beset with problems in nations and parties to the international regulations, complying with 'freer' trading and major difficulties in reaching any consensus on the meaning of 'fairer' trade. As such, the international trade regulatory system is always contentious and dynamic, with different forces propelling its development at different times throughout its history.

2. A Matter of Perception

On its surface, the international trade regulatory system is currently under stress, if not in crisis, and is facing its biggest challenges since the establishment of the GATT in 1947. While factors causing the problems might be identified, they are different at different times. In other words, difficulties and problems in international trade regulation should be understood from a historical perspective and as being issues encountered in a process of continuing evolution. From this perspective, history might be accelerating at the moment, with various government responses to the coronavirus pandemic further revealing many weaknesses of the existing system and challenging many assumptions for free trade and investment. However, any doomsday proclamation of the coming end of globalisation is premature, failing to recognise the resilience of international economic order that is supported by some highly sophisticated institutions and mechanisms for global trade (and investment).

The reality is that this is not the first time that the post-War international economic order (the regulation of international trade being a major part of it) faces some serious challenges. The post-War international economic order, loosely maintained by the Bretton Woods Institutions, was established by Western powers. The foundation of it is liberal market ideologies. It is, however, important to note that the seeds for contention had been sown from the very beginning, for the world was soon to become multi-polar and Western domination was, with the passing of time, to face increasing challenges. Thus, the history of struggle in search of a post-War international economic order, especially international trade regulation, is thus first one between the East and the West and then largely between the North and the South. Suffice it to say that, until the economic rise of Asia, especially China, few credible challenges were ever mounted against the post-War international economic order, with globalisation (principally propelled by global trade and investment) advancing largely unabated until very recently.

In the last two decades or so, China has been at the centre of talks on geopolitics in international relationships and globalisation. At the beginning, the focus was on accommodating the emerging powers (China, India, etc.) and, then, on rebalancing global geopolitical order after the implementation of the Belt and Road Initiative (BRI) by the Chinese government and, mostly recently, the so-called 'decoupling' from China or 're-shoring'/'friend shoring'. Nevertheless, China will continue to be at the centre in the post Covid-19 world order, but the focal points will not be the same. The world shortage, especially in the initial stage of the Covid pandemic, of medical equipment and health products (such as face masks) and the lack of quality control of these imported products (largely from China) have now led to questioning globalisation and the reliability of supply chains in global manufacture. The heavy reliance on China as a market and as a world factory will be, and are being, reviewed by all Western countries, and this must be understood in the context that China's relationship with some Western countries had already been strained before the current crisis. In short, the presumption that China (as a manufacturer) is not replaceable is being questioned and, it is increasingly recognised that China as a market (trade and investment) needs others as much as others need China. 'Decoupling' of the West from China is most unlikely, but re-balancing the trade relations and diversification will occur, as they are already occurring.

Equally profound are the long-term ramifications of the 'temporary' government responses to the Covid crisis such as the massive bailout of business entities and employment in liberal market economies, and the various measures restricting the free flow of people and goods. These measures question the very foundational theories and notions for free trade and globalisation, such as comparative advantage, specialisation, global supply chains, product life cycle and so on. They have also led to the resurfacing of ugly nationalism in the form of demands for self-sufficiency or self-reliance, notions that have long been rejected in Western countries. Covid-19 thus serves as a catalyst, but not a cause in itself, that might accelerate uncertain changes that were seen as unlikely until very recently.

All these difficulties and problems throughout history are well recognised and analysed by scholars and practitioners. There is an extensive body of scholarship on ideological struggles, the rise of developing countries, geopolitical contest, the emerging powers (especially China), the use, misuse or abuse of trading rules and so on. There is however, a lack of a single concise research book that synthesises these underlying causes and factors into a coherent and precise analytical theme. This book attempts to fill this research gap by building upon the existing scholarship and placing the various tensions and conflicts in a perspective that treats them as dynamic factors that have propelled a continuing process of evolution of international trade regulation, rather than seeing them merely as disruptive factors that impair the regulation of global trade.

In short, this book offers a perspective on the evolution of international trade regulation since the end of WWII, in a broad context of international economic order and, on the basis of this perspective, to suggest that regulatory reform, not rejection, is needed to ensure that the present 'pushing-back' against globalisation will not mean the end of globalisation.

3. Structure of the Book

This book starts with Chapter 1 on the foundations of GATT/WTO and the Post-War international economic order. It will first examine the circumstances under which GATT arose as part of the post-War development strategy and the then-prevailing view that conflicts in international trade were also factors contributing to the outbreak of World War II. It will review the theoretical foundation for the post-War international economic order and analyse the fundamental approaches to, and basic principles in, international trade regulation. This chapter will continue to examine the expansion of the international regulatory system through the 'magic' notion of 'trade-related' (measures) and its inherited contradiction: pursuing free trade while insisting on regulating 'trade-related' issues, such as intellectual protection, trade-related investment measures and, more recently, environmental protection, climate change and other 'social issues'. While the inclusion of 'trade-related' measures in the WTO regulatory system seems to suggest that the international trade regulation is an ever-expanding system, it is also suggested that it is more useful to consider international trade regulation as a dynamic system that is not only expanding but also 'harmonising' with the UN efforts to secure world peace and economic prosperity – the original idea in the immediate post-War period when the Bretton Woods conference was convened. In this context, while the inclusion of 'trade-related' measures in the WTO has sown the seeds for tension and conflict, it also ensures that the included measures are now subject to dispute resolution with economic sanctions (in contrast to political conflict). Through these analyses and examination of the various challenges throughout the history of international trade regulation since the end of WWII, this chapter will demonstrate that the international trade regulatory system, unlike many other international treaties, is always meant to be a 'living' system that would evolve throughout time to meet new challenges, and to resolve tensions and conflicts at a given time.

Chapter 2 will examine the first major challenge to the international trade regulatory regime – the special needs of developing countries and the demand for a New International Economic Order (NIEO), as a result of rapid decolonisation in many parts of the world and the rise of several Asian developing countries (especially the four 'Asian Tigers'). The demand for an NIEO or the cry for a fairer and more equitable trading system then led to the insertion of Part IV into GATT and, eventually, the development of a 'Special and Differential Treatment' (S&D) system for developing nations in the GATT/WTO. Subsequent to this development, it emerged that, if the initial West-East tensions did not lead to major conflicts in international trade regulation, the South-North tensions did cause some major frictions among trading nations and served as a dynamic that continues to propel new development of the system. Nevertheless, careful examination of the movement towards fairer trade in recognition of different trading capacities of nations and in response to the special needs of developing countries suggests that, until now, a fairer and equitable order exists only on paper, but such a movement does question whether the theoretical foundation of international trade regulation should be modified and, if so, how.

Chapter 3 changes focus from the global trade regulatory system to its 'side' development – the rapidly developing regional trade agreements (RTAs). It first reviews, briefly, the development of RTAs under GATT/WTO, highlighting certain notable features of the development. It then focuses on the context in which the 'super' RTAs have emerged and been negotiated. It concludes that the rapid and substantive development of RTAs, though not fundamentally undermining the foundation of GATT/WTO, significantly fracture the supposedly global regulatory regime and, as such, seriously undermines multilateralism. It further concludes that, in the final analysis, the recent RTA development, first the Trans-Pacific Partnership/Comprehensive and Progressive Agreement for Trans-Pacific Partnership (TPP/CPTPP), the Regional Comprehensive Economic Partnership (RCEP), and now the Indo-Pacific Economic Framework (IPEF), has led to increasing geopolitical tensions, if not conflict.

Chapter 4 continues the discussion of Chapter 3 but moves the focus to the unprecedented challenges to the liberal foundation of the multilateral trade regime posed by the rise of China. While the rise of China raises many complicated and complex questions, two prominent strategies are likely to have major impact on the liberal international economic order. These are

China's 'One Belt One Road' Initiative (BRI) and its increasing use of economic powers against countries that do not always agree with its geopolitical objectives. The more recent 'decoupling' (from China) talk in some Western countries has been, so far, a non-starter, but the needs for diversification are now widely felt globally, reflecting the on-going geopolitical struggles as well as market forces.

This chapter thus first analyses the BRI as investment projects and as a geopolitical strategy. It then examines China's geo-economic manoeuvre in BRI and in international relations more generally, as well as the so-called 'decoupling' 'strategy' in the geopolitical and geo-economic struggle. It concludes that there is yet no sign of the end of the geopolitical struggle between China and the existing powers led by the US, but it is also argued that it is better to see the rise of China as yet another dynamic force that has to be accommodated and, through accommodation, that should be channeled into the efforts to reform international trade regulation.

The final chapter is premised on the view that the survival of a clear, reliable and yet flexible international trade regulation system depends on an efficient and effective dispute resolution mechanism, not a rigid system of trade rules. It first reviews, very briefly, the dispute resolution mechanisms under the GATT. It then moves to analyse the same under the WTO, focusing on the improvement made at the Uruguay Round of negotiations. In particular, the current dispute resolution problems and the proposed reforms are closely examined. This chapter then proceeds to analyse issues that are not covered by the WTO dispute resolution mechanisms but often cause major trade problems in our contemporary world. This chapter concludes that a resolution to the current impasse as well as disputes augmenting the current WTO mechanisms is critical, if the multilateral trade regime is to survive the various challenges it now faces.

This book ends with a conclusion that the dynamic trade regulation system will continue to evolve and survive the various challenges, if its history is any guide. Critically, the global regulatory regime must be understood as a dynamic system as well as a result of a proper balancing of interests. However, such a balance is constantly challenging when new issues and powers emerge. As such, a never-ending cycle of evolution is the natural movement of this dynamic yet stable system. As such, emerging or other new powers need to be accommodated, through reform, not rejection.

1 Freer Trade

GATT/WTO and the Foundation of Post-War International Economic Order

1. Introduction

Trade, in a broad sense, has been with us since time immemorial; it is perhaps as old as human civilisation and existed well before the notion of modern statehood. Although the term 'free trade' is frequently used, trade is always regulated and, not infrequently protected. The existence of, since medieval times, and compliance by traders with, the *Lex mercatoria* – a body of customs and usages of international trade as well as mechanisms for dispute resolution (see Schill, 2014) suggest that sophisticated trade regulation has existed for a long history in our civilisation.

Ever since the emergence of the notion of nationhood, all established national borders have been controlled and international trade regulated for such purposes as revenue raising, the protection of domestic industries, or national security and/or health. In this context, the first thing to undertake in order to achieve 'free trade' is, ironically, to use regulation to remove trade barriers or even trade prohibitions (see Kindleberger, 1973). However, a modern and truly multilateral trade system is a product of post-World War II efforts at economic reconstruction and cooperation among nations.

Regulation and free trade are two inherently contradictory terms. The more regulation we have the less free trade would be; and conversely, the less regulation then the more likely or more easily trade barriers might be imposed and/or existing regulations might be abused or misused. In the post-War period and despite setbacks, the movement is, in general, towards more regulation that aims at removing trade barriers as well as ensuring compliance with the established rules. In other words, the evolving regulatory regime aims to establish freer and fairer trade through increasingly complicated and sophisticated regulations.

This chapter examines the emergence of the post-War international trade regulatory regime, principally in the form of the General Agreement on Tariffs and Trade/World Trade Organization (GATT/WTO). The focus of this chapter is on the nature and development of this regulatory regime.

DOI: 10.4324/9781003275510-2

2. The Emergence of the Post-War International Trade Regulatory Regime

One of the most significant post-War developments was the establishment, in June 1945, of the United Nations (UN) to replace the ineffective League of Nations. While the most important task of the UN is to prevent future wars by maintaining peace and security throughout the world, it is however important too to recognise that the UN is also to promote international economic and social cooperation, as evidenced in the title of Chapter 9 of the UN Charter (International Economic and Social Co-operation). Details of its functions in this regard are set out in Art 55 of the UN Charter, which include the promotion of 'solutions of international economic, social, health, and related problems; and international cultural and educational co-operation.' (Art 55 (b) of the UN Charter).

The inclusion of international economic and social cooperation in the UN's fundamental tasks reflected one of the main strands of thinking about the possible causes of World War II at the end of that War. A prominent WTO scholar has pointed out that

> the mistakes concerning economic policy during the interwar period (1920–1940) were a major cause of the disasters that led to the WWII. . . . During this interwar period, nations, particularly after the damaging 1930 US Tariff Act, took many protectionist measures, including quota-type restrictions, which choked off international trade. Political leaders of the US and elsewhere made statements about the importance of establishing post-war economic institutions that would prevent these mistakes from happening again.
>
> (Jackson, 1989: 31)

Thus, an international conference sponsored by ministries of finance was held in 1944 in Bretton Woods, New Hampshire, in the United States. This meeting established the International Monetary Fund (IMF) and the International Bank for Reconstruction and Development (IBRD, the World Bank), both of which then became a part of the UN structure. Although the GATT was not formed at the 1944 Bretton Woods Conference, the Bretton Woods Conference nevertheless contemplated the necessity of an International Trade Organisation (ITO as it was then referred to) (Jackson, 1989: 27–28; Skubik, 1993: 417–418).[1]

1 For this reason, the Bretton Woods institutions are often referred to as including IMF, World Bank, and the GATT/WTO.

After the founding of the UN in 1945, the establishment of a world trade institution to complement the IMF and the World Bank was one of the very earliest agenda items of the UN. In February 1946 at the UN Economic and Social Council's (ECOSOC's) first meeting, a resolution calling for a conference to draft a charter for an International Trade Organisation (ITO) was adopted, and draft work started almost immediately (Jackson, 1989: 32). At the UN Conference on Trade and Employment, held from 21 November 1947 to 24 March 1948 in Havana, the ITO charter was completed under which the International Trade Organisation was to be established as the third pillar in the institutional structure of specialised UN agencies. Together they were to promote post-war economic reconstruction by way of funding major development, maintaining currency stability, and growing global trade (Sarcevic, 1990: 210).

The ITO of course never came into existence when the US failed to approve it despite the US having earlier taken the principal initiative to develop the ITO charter in the first place.[2] Nevertheless, major provisions on reciprocal reduction of tariffs and general clauses on tariff in the original ITO charter were revised and, on the basis of these revised provisions, the GATT was born. In recognising the urgent needs for such an agreement and in order to avoid potential difficulties or delays in national legislatures as well as to facilitate the approval by executive governments (see Jackson, 1989: 32–37), the GATT was to be merely a multilateral treaty, not an organisation and, was only brought into operation by the Protocol of Provisional Application (PPA). In other words, the GATT was meant to be a temporary agreement, pending further development to establish the ITO. As the GATT was to complement the post-War international economic institutions, it was no surprise that the GATT was soon transformed from a *de jure* temporary agreement with contracting parties into a *de facto* institution (Jackson, 1989: 37), where new issues and problems in global trade are discussed and addressed, and disputes among members are settled.

This unusual birth of GATT means that efforts continued to be made to complete the unfinished task of establishing an international trade organisation and, ultimately, such a task was completed some 50 years later when the Marrakesh Agreement Establishing the World Trade Organization Agreement was signed by members in April 1994 and the WTO was formally established on 1 January 1995. Also because of this unusual birth, the

2 During the 1954–55 Review Session, a second attempt was made and a charter for Organisation for Trade Cooperation (OTC) was drafted, but failed to be adopted (Jackson, 1989: 31).

GATT (as a *de facto* organisation) and, later, WTO (as a *de jure* organisation), became a multilateral organisation outside the UN system.[3]

3. The Liberal Foundation of the Post-War International Economic Order

As world politics in the post-War period was dominated by the United States and its allies, the Bretton Woods system is, unsurprisingly, a product of Western powers. With the US being the then-economic hegemon, the global economic order that the Bretton Woods System pursued was a liberal economic order.[4] In this liberal order, we are reminded, the 'pride of place is given to market rationality', even though '[t]his is not to say that authority is absent from such an order. It is to say that authority relations are constructed in such a way as to give maximum scope to market forces rather than to constrain them' (Ruggie, 1982: 381). In other words, the post-War international economic order was founded on a liberal market ideology that places its faith on market rationality while limiting government roles to, essentially, foster such a market order. This ideology is most clearly reflected in the GATT approach to trade liberalisation and regulation – free and open market under transparent regulation and operating on a non-discriminatory basis.[5] Like most trade theories or justifications for free trade, the liberal market ideology that underpins the pursuit of the post-War international economic order has been criticised and challenged from time to time,[6] and different narratives have been advanced through history (Cohen, 2019). However, the liberal economic order is not an abstract notion that could easily be discarded; it is embedded in the underlying principles of international economic institutions, as will be further shown through the more detailed examination of the specific institutions of the Bretton Woods system later.

3 The UN website lists the WTO as its 'related organisation' (see www.un.org/en/about-us/un-system (last accessed 18/10/21)), but the WTO lists the UN as one of its main partners for collaboration (see www.wto.org/english/thewto_e/coher_e/coher_e.htm (last accessed 18/10/21)), but it is not formally a part of the UN.

4 On the relationship between liberal economic order and the existence of a dominant economic power (an economic hegemon), see Keohane, 1980. This liberal economic order is, of course, part of the liberal international order established post-War by the US and its allies. See Jahn, 2018; Ruggie, 1982. There is of course a large body of literature on liberal international order. For a literature survey on the topic, see Amadi, 2020.

5 In other words, trade, just like the market economy, is not one that is only regulated by the 'invisible hands' of the market; it aims at freer trade that is regulated.

6 These are discussed in the following chapters of the book.

The principal functions of the IMF were, and (despite fundamental changes in international monetary practice) still largely remain, to eliminate foreign exchange restrictions, stabilise currency exchange rates, and facilitate the balance of payments. The World Bank, as a sister organisation to the IMF, is designed to finance major development projects in member countries (Cheeseman, 1992: 1257), with a focus nowadays on developing countries. Although the primary concern of the World Bank is the promotion of investment, it nevertheless has a function to 'promote the long-range balanced growth of international trade' (Art 1 (iii) of the IBRD Articles of Agreement). Indeed, the World Bank finances imports of member countries that are vital to the development of a particular sector or the economy as a whole (Sarcevic, 1990: 210). Structurally, the World Bank is a group with subsidiary organisations fulfilling its various functions.[7] The relationship between the Bank and the IMF is that no country can become a member of the World Bank and receive its 'loans' unless it is also a member of the IMF.

Although initially the IMF and the World Bank were meant to serve all members, for the larger part of their history they were mainly utilised by developing countries in tackling deteriorating balances of payments and infrastructure development problems. However, they became controversial when the IMF began to impose conditions on borrowing countries for the use of its 'loans' – the so-called 'conditionality' practice – which conditions are almost always also imposed by the World Bank.[8] Since the 1980s, the World Bank has also provided structural adjustment loans for the adjustment of industry, agriculture and labour to changes in the international economy (Sarcevic, 1990: 210). These conditions and requirements for structural adjustment were all geared towards establishing market economies and reducing the role of government in economic management and, as such, to facilitate the establishment of a liberal world economic order (Islam, 1999: 69–70; Sarcevic, 1990: 210).

The principal objectives of the GATT are framed in terms of 'raising standards of living, ensuring full employment and a large and steadily

7 These subsidiary organisations of the World Bank include the International Bank for Reconstruction and Development (World Bank – the principal body of the World Bank Group (WBG)); the International Finance Corporation; the International Development Association; the Multilateral Investment Guarantee Agency; and the International Centre for Settlement of Investment Disputes (ICSID). Beside the World Bank, there are also several regional development banks: the African Development Bank, the Asian Development Bank, the Arab Fund for Economic and Social Development, the Caribbean Development Bank, the European Investment Bank, and the Inter-American Development Bank (Cheeseman, 1992: 1257).

8 For a summary of the 'conditionality' practice, see Skubik, 1993: 425; Islam, 1999: 69–70.

growing volume of real income and effective demand, developing the full use of the resources of the world and expanding the production and exchange of goods'. The means to achieve these objectives is to use 'reciprocal and mutually advantageous arrangements directed to the substantial reduction of tariffs and other barriers to trade and to the elimination of discriminatory treatment in international commerce' (Preamble of GATT 1947). In other words, the GATT is to reduce trade barriers (principally tariffs) (or in other words, trade liberalisation) and to eliminate discrimination between members.

Although the regulatory objectives seem to be straightforward, the GATT is not a simple nor a single agreement; it is a complex and evolving body of agreements, which include the principal agreement (the 1947 General Agreement on Tariffs and Trade), the Protocol of Provisional Application (PPA), Annexes, Schedules, protocols (accession agreements), subsequent agreements that amend, modify or elaborate the 1947 GATT provisions including some that are in the form of a stand-alone 'code of conduct'.

Although this framework of agreements is a complex (and eventually complicated) structure, containing various principles, operational rules and exceptions, it is designed to, essentially, address the following issues:[9]

(1) tariff reduction/trade liberalisation: to ensure the reduction of tariffs through concessions negotiated among and committed to by members (Art II and Schedules);
(2) non-discrimination: to ensure the elimination of discrimination through the most-favoured nation treatment (MFN) (Art I), national treatment (NA) (Art III), and other non-discrimination provisions;
(3) technical barriers: to address selected technical barriers that are lawful but could also impede free trade, including antidumping and countervailing duties (Art VI); valuation of goods for customs purposes (Art VII); procedures of customs administration (Art VIII & X); marks of origin (Art IX); quantitative restrictions (Art XI); subsidies (Art XVI); and state trading monopolies (Art XVII);
(4) exceptions: to allow certain exceptions that are necessary for the security, wellbeing, public order or morale in the member states;
(5) negotiation and dispute resolution: to provide a forum for continuing negotiation (hence evolution of the agreements) and dispute resolution (principally by negotiation); and
(6) developing countries: to provide special and preferential treatment to developing countries through Part IV (Arts XXVI–XXXVIII) of GATT (which were added in 1964) and additional agreements.

9 For more detailed categories of the constitutive texts and functions, see McGovern, 1986: 4–5.

In other words, GATT is to address border control measures in a non-discriminatory manner, with a clear objective of increasing and expanding international trade (initially of goods, but much later, of services as well).

Border control is established by all nations for a variety of reasons, and there is no intention to eliminate all control measures, either for goods, services or movement of persons. However, border measures that would impede international trade to a varied degree and some identified measures are dealt with by the GATT, though not in a uniform manner. In fact, there is a huge discrepancy in terms of the regulation or elimination of the different border control measures and, for the purpose of illustration, is summarised here:[10]

Principal Border Control Measures	*Extent of Regulation*
Tariffs (Arti II)	to continue but to be reduced
Quotas (Arts X & XIII)	to be prohibited
Subsidies (Art XVI)	disciplines to be strengthened
State trading (Art XVII)	disciplines to be strengthened
Customs procedures	norms of reasonableness

Structurally, Art I on most-favoured-nation treatment and Art II on tariffs form Part I of the GATT, the revision of which requires unanimity among members which then suggests the importance of tariff reduction and the principle of non-discrimination. National treatment (Art III) and disciplines (sometimes referred to as code of conduct) on other potential technical barriers (also referred to as 'non-tariff measures', such as the use of antidumping and countervailing duties, valuation of goods for customs purposes, procedures of customs administration, marks of origin, quantitative restrictions, subsidies and State trading monopolies) form other specific and substantive obligations of members.[11]

Without entering into detailed analysis, it is necessary to highlight the following points. First, tariff and quotas are specific and definite quantitative restrictions that are easy to identify, but other trade restrictive measures are not of the same nature and the regulation over them is very difficult and

10 These were the five types of border barriers (and their corresponding regulation) said to have been the focus of the drafters of the GATT. See Jackson, 1989: 115–116. Obviously, they are by no means the only trade barriers. Indeed, members have been, ever since the implementation of GATT, using the various GATT-allowed exceptions and trade remedies as technical barriers to imports.

11 On tariff reduction and its achievement, see WTO Tariffs (undated). However, with the success of tariff reduction, non-tariff trade barriers soon became the new focus in trade negotiation as well as causes of major disputes among members.

not to be rigid. On the other hand, however, this lack of rigid regulation also allows for evolution and development. Secondly, many of the initial obligations imposed on member countries were not clearly defined and were soon to cause complications in their operation as well as cause disputes among, and abuse or misuse by, members. It can be asserted that this trade regulation regime was designed to evolve and expand, with details and clarity to be worked out through its evolution and, as such, its objectives would be difficult to be achieved without an efficient and effective dispute resolution mechanism.

Non-discrimination, a typical liberal trading idea and a core principle of the international trade regulatory regime (Wolff, 2019), is to be achieved through the age-old principle of most-favoured-nation treatment (MFN).[12] The increasingly important national treatment principles, and other non-discrimination requirements are contained in specific provisions of the GATT and its subsequent agreements.

Specifically, MFN treatment, though not an especially favourable treatment as might be suggested by its wording, demands equal treatment for like-products from all members with respect to customs duties and charges as well as rules and formalities imposed at the national borders (Art I of GATT). However, Art I contains some very complicated provisions including exceptions that could be made on account of preferential arrangement and free trade (including customs union), developing countries, code conditionality[13] and so on. The overall effect of the complex provisions is in fact to limit the application of the MFN treatment to circumstances defined by the GATT.[14]

National Treatment, on the other hand, requires equal treatment of domestic and imported products of a similar nature with respect to internal taxes and charges as well as laws, regulations and other requirements affecting the sales, transport, distribution, use and so on of the imported products. Its principal intention is 'to provide equal conditions of competition once goods had been cleared through customs' (Jackson, 1989: 190). As alluded to earlier, with the reduction of tariffs, national treatment is gaining an increasing importance in international trade. Similar to

12 It is said that MFN treatment has a long history that can be traced back to the twelfth century (although the phrase seems to have first appeared in the seventeenth century). See Jackson, 1989: 133.

13 This so-called 'code conditionality' means that the benefits of a stand-alone code treatment will not be granted to members who have not accepted the code.

14 Practically every aspect of this Article has now been interpreted many times by GATT/WTO dispute resolution mechanism. The best and most comprehensive source on the interpretation and jurisprudence of GATT and WTO is the WTO Analytical Index.

the MFN treatment, exceptions to the principle are allowed in relation to such conduct as government procurement and cinematograph films (Art III (8) of the GATT), and the various aspects of requirements and exceptions have been extensively interpreted by GATT/WTO dispute resolution mechanism.

Additionally, some GATT provisions specifically require contracting parties not to discriminate against any other contracting parties. For instance, Art XIII specifically requires that a contracting party should not discriminate against any other contracting party in the administration of import or export quantitative restrictions.

Again, it should be stressed that, although liberalism was the foundation of the GATT, it is clear that the principal and supporting agreements were and still are, however, not about absolute free trade. Other than the clear provisions on tariff reduction, the elimination of quotas, and (qualified) non-discriminatory treatment, disciplines in other areas of trade barriers are far from being strict. When stricter disciplines are established in these areas, they are often in the form of separate agreements (codes of conduct) whose acceptance is not compulsory. Further, similar to most international treaties, the GATT also contains a long list of exceptions, ranging from general exceptions (to allow government to implement its general public order or public health and welfare policies) and national security (to allow governments to protect their essential security interests) to the more specific exceptions such as measures to rectify severe problems in balance of payments, preferential arrangements in customs union or free trade agreements and many more. Even the core principle of the GATT/WTO – the MFN treatment – the obligations are not absolute, as has just been pointed out previously.

The exceptions and provisions that only provide less than clear and strict disciplines on many non-tariff measures are clearly the sources that create difficulties and ineffectiveness in trade regulation as well as disputes among contracting parties. However, they do not change the nature of the GATT. After all, GATT is not about absolute free trade, rather, the aim of GATT is to generate a more open/transparent and secure trading climate enabling each member to compete with others with fewer artificial trade barriers (Islam, 1993: 226), and thus to secure freer and fairer trade.

In short, the approach to the regulation of international trade, represented by the cornerstone provisions of the first three articles on the reduction of tariffs and the non-discriminatory treatment among contracting members, is a reflection of liberalism in nature, that everyone is to be treated equally for the goal of liberalisation of international trade, or in other words, the typical liberal idea of freer trade and competition on equal footing is embedded in the GATT as its ideological foundation.

4. GATT as an Evolving Mechanism

As a temporary agreement that made use of a portion of a much more comprehensive package to regulate trade and which contains many vague disciplines on many non-tariff measures, it is not surprising that GATT, though having a reasonably narrow focus on trade in goods, was meant to be further developed. Indeed, upon the signing of GATT in October 1947, Contracting Parties met almost every six months, discussing not only problems about the implementation of GATT rules but also the unfinished business – the establishment of an Organisation for Trade Cooperation. In any case, the specific and binding tariff concessions committed by members under the Schedules were subject to periodic negotiations under GATT,[15] but, more importantly, the need for improvement of GATT rules was felt strongly during the early 1950s and, hence, the ninth regular session, scheduled for 1954–55, was designated as a review session.[16] As such, the GATT was also to serve as a forum for negotiation and discussion and, hence, as a *de facto* organisation (as well as a mechanism for resolution of disputes).

As a temporary agreement (until 1995 when WTO came into existence) that was subject to continuing negotiations, the GATT is unique in international law; it is not a static but a dynamic system, constantly evolving throughout its history.[17] As a set of agreements, nothing therein was meant to be set in stone and almost everything thereunder was meant to be re-negotiated periodically and interpreted by the rather vague dispute resolution mechanisms. These re-negotiations then resulted in many more agreements that amended, supplemented or clarified the original agreements since 1947.[18] Importantly, as illustrated by the following table, GATT negotiation scope was gradually broadened, especially at the Uruguay Round (1986–1993).[19] As such, it also eventually became controversial as to the legitimate ambit of the GATT 'jurisdiction'.

15 Under the 1955 revised Art XXVIII, a member can in fact modify or withdraw tariff concessions at regular intervals of three years.

16 At this session, a plan, a much less ambitious one than that for the ITO, to establish an Organisation for Trade Cooperation as an institutional framework was drafted, but again failed to get the approval of the US Congress. See Jackson, 1989: 37–38.

17 Of course, this is also true of the WTO agreements, though their development has suffered some major setback in the failure of the Doha Round of negotiations.

18 Technically, amending the GATT is governed by Art XXX of the GATT, under which, amendments to Arts I (MFN), II (Tariff) and XXIX (relation with Havana Charter) of GATT require, theoretically, unanimous acceptance. Amending the remainder of GATT requires two-thirds acceptance on the part of all contracting parties, but such an amendment obligates only those CPs which accept it. For more detailed discussion, see Jackson, 1989: 51.

19 The Uruguay Round will be further discussed later.

GATT Negotiation Rounds and the Expansion of Negotiation Scope[20]

Round	*Year*	*Participating Members*	*Discussions*
(1)	Geneva 1947	23	Tariffs
(2)	Annecy 1949	13	Tariffs
(3)	Torquay 1950	38	Tariffs
(4)	Geneva 1956	26	Tariffs
(5)	Dillon 1960–1	26	Tariffs
(6)	Kennedy 1962–7	62	Tariffs, Anti-dumping, developing countries
(7)	Tokyo 1973–9	102	Tariffs, Non-Tariffs & 'framework' agreements
(8)	Uruguay 1986–93	123	WTO, Agriculture, Textiles, Services, Intellectual Property Rights, Investment, DR, etc.

The above table suggests that, except the 'review session' of 1954–55 (GATT, 1954), the initial five rounds of negotiations focused on reducing tariffs,[21] and, by and large, the negotiations were hugely successful.

Tariffs are the most transparent trade barriers, but its utility as a trade regulatory mechanism is limited once the average of tariffs is reduced to a certain level where it then serves a function similar to a sales tax and no more. Not surprisingly, by the time of the Kennedy Round of 1962–7, it was realised that the tariff reduction on industrial products had reached its limit and that non-tariff barriers hence became more important in liberalisation of global trade and, thus, negotiation focus began to shift to non-tariff issues. Despite the unfortunate domination of the dispute between the US and the then-European Economic Community over farmers' subsidies, the Kennedy Round achieved the first major side-agreement – the 1967 Antidumping Code – and began negotiations on issues specifically for developing countries (Jackson, 1989: 54), thus signifying the shift of trade regulation from reduction of tariffs to non-tariff measures as trade barriers.

20 See Awuku, 1994: 77; and WTO GATT Years (undated). The WTO is meant to continue the practice of 'rounds of negotiation' However, the WTO has been much less successful and its first ever Round (the Doha Round), launched in 2001 as a Development Round (initially participated by 155 Contracting Parties) was unceremoniously ended in 2015 when Members failed to reach a consensus on continuing multilateral trade negotiations under the framework of the Doha Round (DFAT (undated)). There has since been no more new rounds of negotiation launched by the WTO, although *ad hoc* negotiations continue at the WTO.

21 On tariffs, a similar statement can also be made in relation to the WTO negotiations. See WTO 20 Years (undated).

Building upon the limited achievement at the Kennedy Round, the seventh Tokyo Round produced some far-reaching and substantive side-agreements and stand-alone codes of conduct in relation to technical barriers to trade, government procurement, subsidies, customs valuation, import licensing procedures, anti-dumping and so on.[22] It also reached a further consensus (in the form of an Understanding) on preferential treatment for developing countries, trade measures taken for balance-of-payments purposes, safeguard action for development purposes and dispute resolution. Together, the overall impact of these results was to substantially broaden the scope of coverage of the GATT system (Jackson, 1989: 55),[23] but all subject matters were still comfortably within the original ambit of GATT.

5. Seeds of Contention: The Uruguay Round and a Transformed System

5.1. Transformation and Expansion

With one notable exception (the preferential treatment for developing countries), the first seven rounds of negotiations and their results can be seen as fundamentally in the nature of making improvements to the original design of the GATT. The fundamentals of the GATT, that is, its regulatory scope and its fundamental approach to regulation, remain essentially the same despite the huge increase of its membership (referred to as Contracting Parties) throughout the years. The next round of negotiation, the Eighth (and final) Round (the Uruguay Round) under the GATT, then was going to have much more profound implications for trade regulation, even though, as will be shown later, the liberal foundation of GATT has remained largely intact.

The Uruguay Round of Multilateral Trade Negotiation is described as 'the most complex and ambitious programme of negotiations ever undertaken by GATT' (Stewart, 1993: 1). From the decision to launch the Round of negotiations on 22 September 1986 to the final adoption of the results of the Round at the end of 1993 (though only officially signed in April 1994), it took over 2,500 days of negotiations between 117 countries to produce a 550-page final agreement: an average of five days a page (EC, 1994: 5). The result of the Uruguay Round is described as 'an outstanding achievement and a landmark in the history of the international trading systems of the world' (Rom, 1994: 5). It indeed signals the beginning of a new era for

22 Not all GATT members are contracting parties to these codes and agreements.

23 Such an expansion also creates a legal problem, that is, the legal status of these side-agreements and understandings became controversial (see Jackson, 1989: 56).

international trade regulation and, as a result of this major expansion of regulatory scope, the GATT itself becomes only a part of the new package of agreements dealing with international trade.

In essence, changes brought about by the conclusion of the Uruguay Round are transformative and expansionist in nature, each reinforces the other.

First, GATT as a *de facto* organisation was transformed into a *de jure* one when the WTO was officially established on 1 January 1995. The establishment of the WTO finally completes the Bretton Woods structure as it was originally designed some 50 years earlier. It is however important to stress again that, while the World Bank and the IMF are specialised agencies of the UN, the WTO is not part of the UN. Specifically, the WTO-UN relationship is governed by the 'Arrangements for Effective Cooperation with other Intergovernmental Organizations-Relations Between the WTO and the United Nations' of 1995,[24] which determines that there are 'no grounds for formal institutional links between the WTO and the United Nations', but there is 'the need for the establishment of cooperative ties between the two organizations'. Also unique in the case of the WTO being an inter-governmental organisation, members need not be sovereign states, even though the WTO and its officials and representatives enjoy similar privileges and immunities stipulated in the Convention on the Privileges and Immunities of the Specialized Agencies, approved by the General Assembly of the United Nations on 21 November 1947 (Art VIII of the WTO Agreement).

An important feature of the WTO is, other than members of the 1947 GATT as at the conclusion of the Uruguay Round of negotiation, a country or a region wishing to join the WTO will need to undertake a very lengthy and extremely complicated process of negotiation with all other members. Another unique feature of the WTO, in terms of negotiation, is its practice of the formation of groups among members with shared interests. In this practice, groups often have their own coordinators that speak with a unified voice for their groups,[25] though some groups are more active and more economically powerful than others. These features add additional complexity to negotiations.

Secondly, in addition to a systematic review and improvement of the then-GATT provisions, the Uruguay Round went far beyond the traditional subjects of liberalisation of trade through reduction of tariffs and elimination

24 A copy of the Arrangement is available at https://docs.wto.org/dol2fe/Pages/SS/directdoc.aspx?filename=q:/WT/GC/W10.pdf&Open=True (last accessed 18/10/21).

25 For an updated list of groups, see www.wto.org/english/tratop e/dda_e/negotiating_groups_e.htm (last accessed 20/10/21).

of non-tariff trade barriers. It introduced some entirely new subjects, such as trade in services (the General Agreement on Trade in Services, GATS), trade-related intellectual property rights (the Agreement on Trade-Related Aspects of Intellectual Property Rights, TRIPS), and trade-related investment measures (the Agreement on Trade-Related Investment Measures, TRIMS).

The results of the Uruguay Round form a complex structure of agreements, which are divided into multilateral trade agreements, plurilateral trade agreements and various declarations and decisions. Importantly, under each category, there is effectively a package of agreements, rather than a single instrument. Further, among this plethora of agreements, the multilateral trade agreements form an integral part of the WTO Agreement and bind all members, and only a small number of agreements are categorised as the plurilateral trade agreements which are optional for members. The practical difference between them is that, in the acceptance of or accession to the WTO Agreement, a member must accept all agreements which are integral parts of the WTO Agreement but a member has an option to determine whether to accept any plurilateral agreement which is also administered by the WTO.[26] The point here is that WTO agreements are extremely complex and complicated, and their acceptance is, for most of the agreements, compulsory for all members. As a result, its further evolution is much more difficult to make than it was under the GATT.

Finally, and not surprisingly, major reforms were made to the GATT dispute resolution mechanism. The result is that the weak, negotiation/consultation-based, compromise-intended GATT dispute resolution mechanism, which had been criticised for long delays, inconsistencies, uncertainties, inadequacy of enforcement and so on. (Kohona, 1994: 24), was transformed into a rule-based adjudication-style mechanism that specifically addresses many problems that had plagued the original GATT mechanism. Although many problems were to emerge in the years since the establishment of the WTO, it is a much superior mechanism than its predecessor. Indeed, until recently, it is often referred to as WTO's 'Crown Jewel'.[27] As will be discussed in Chapter 5, in an ever-expanding system of regulation under an ever-increasingly complex and complicated geopolitical circumstance, an efficient and effective dispute resolution mechanism is an indispensable part of a sustainable global system for trade regulation.

26 Art II of the WTO Agreement. In reality, plurilateral agreements have only limited number of acceptances among WTO members.

27 The critical roles of the WTO dispute resolution will be examined in Chapter 5.

5.2. Seeds of Contention

As already alluded to previously, the existence of a large number of exceptions and provisions that only provide less than clear and strict disciplines on many non-tariff measures are the sources of difficulties and ineffectiveness in the GATT regime. The Uruguay Round of negotiations sowed, much deeply, some stronger seeds of contention that are now being realised.

It can be reasonably said that the Uruguay Round was revolutionary in its expansion of the scope of GATT, the establishment of a *de jure* organisation and a hugely improved, adjudication-oriented dispute settlement mechanism. In this context, the Uruguay Round made a great advance towards freer trade. However, the expansion of regulatory scope is not without controversy, and its failure to make GATT/WTO a fairer regulatory system has been criticised by many.[28]

The extension of regulatory scope to cover trade in services was almost inevitable as trade in services had by then become increasingly important for developed nations. At the time of the Uruguay Round, trade in services accounted for 20% to 25% of global trade, but 50–60% of Gross National Product (GNP) in developed countries (Trebilcock, Howse, & Eliason, 2012: 215), and this weight of trade in services in global trade was the principal justification to bring the sector under the umbrella of the GATT[29] and to establish a set of common rules for such trade (EC, 1994: 23). The rapid development of trade in services since then has further justified the need for such regulation: service imports tripled between 1994 to 2004,[30] and in 2019, global services exports were valued at US$6.1 trillion.[31] It is however worth noting that the dominant force in trade in services then was the Western-developed economy while service sectors (such as telecommunication, banking, insurance, etc.) in many developing countries were (and many still are) in very weak, if not precarious and, vulnerable positions against any foreign 'invasion'.

The justification for introducing investment measures and intellectual property protection to the trade regulatory regime was innovative and very different from the regime covering the trade in goods. There was no

28 On this issue, see discussions here and further discussions in Chapter 2.

29 Though taking a similar approach to regulation, trade in services was regulated by a separate agreement. However, it was negotiated under and based on the GATT before the WTO came into existence.

30 See Trebilcock, Howse, & Eliason, 2012: 472, citing an IMF research report.

31 See UNCTAD trade statistics: https://stats.unctad.org/handbook/Services/Total.html (last accessed 21/10/21)

disagreement that measures introduced by hosting governments to attract foreign direct investment, such as tax and other financial incentives, can have important and potentially trade-distorting effects. These so-called trade-related investment measures included non-market factors (or performance requirements), such as local content requirements, export performance requirements, trade balance requirements, technology transfer and licensing requirements, exchange and remittance restrictions, domestic sales requirements, supply of specific goods to certain markets, local equity requirements, product mandating requirements and manufacturing requirements and limitations. Obviously, these were measures that principally existed in developing countries at the time of the Uruguay Round of negotiations and, thus, the inclusion of regulation in these areas principally restricted governments in developing countries in their capacities to determine their industrial policies. Similarly, there was little disagreement that the increasing flow of goods, services and investment has, at the same time, caused the increasing violation of intellectual property rights in technologies, brand names or commercial secrets. Once again, no one would be under any illusion that the new measures were not mainly intended for the protection of intellectual property rights from the developed countries. Further, it was clear that there were no effective disciplinary sanctions against trade-distorting investment measures or the violation of intellectual property rights. However, neither was investment *per se* nor was intellectual property ever covered by GATT regulations. In the case of intellectual property, the UN has already had a specialised agency, the World Intellectual Property Organization (WIPO), which had been operating reasonably well since 1970 when the Convention Establishing the World Intellectual Proper Organisation went into force. There were various justifications, reasoning and analysis for the inclusion of these two subject matters (Symposium on TRIPS and TRIMS, 1991; Trebilcock, Howse, & Eliason, 2012), but ultimately, the 'magic' wand arguing for the inclusion of intellectual property was the phrase 'trade-related' that forged the linkage between these issues and trade within the WTO ambit.

The previous brief examination suggests that the three major areas that had been 'claimed' by the Uruguay Round of negotiations were all of major interest to developed and large developing nations. These nations dominated and still dominate trade in services, most intellectual property rights were and are created in these countries, and investment incentives were principally used by developing countries to compete for foreign investment. This suggests that the expansion of scope for the WTO 'jurisdiction' is largely one-sided but resulted in a round of negotiations that was meant to be a development round. As such, this expansion effectively sowed the seeds for contention and conflict between the developed and large developing nations, and other developing nations. In the areas of intellectual property, it did not take long for the new regime to cause major practical problems in the fight against global pandemic, first against AIDS and more recently Covid-19. It was not just the ambitious expansion of scope in the Uruguay Round that caused difficulties. The new agreements touched the nerve of national sovereignty, would affect the life of most citizens in member states, and blatantly displayed the determination of developed (and some large developing) countries to protect their own economic interests while making few concessions to poorer countries. Not surprisingly, it was at this time that GATT/WTO began to attract major protests around the world.

Further, the justification for inclusion of new subject-matters to the purview of GATT/WTO is not just 'revolutionary'; it effectively opened a 'Pandora's box'. This Pandora's box could (and some would say 'should') lead to the WTO having the ability to regulate social issues (such as human rights and labour conditions), environmental protection, climate change, and many more. For instance, the developed nations[32] had argued that negotiations on trade-related intellectual property (TRIPs) were intended to safeguard intellectual property rights while at the same time ensuring the unimpeded flow of international trade (EC, 1994: 23). If the same logic is applied, one can easily argue that our environment, climate change, human rights and so on, must be safeguarded while ensuring the smooth flow and development of international trade. But if we do so, does it mean that the WTO is going to replace most of the international organisations including the United Nations? Fundamentally, GATT/WTO is about reducing trade barriers in a non-discrimination manner. It is a 'Pandora's box' because GATT/WTO history has suggested, as will be further discussed in the following chapters, that it has never been effective in dealing with issues other than trade barriers.

Despite the expansion of regulatory scope at the Uruguay Round, it should be pointed out that GATT/WTO is largely about the removal of import barriers and has largely neglected export restrictions. This weakness was gravely exposed during the Covid-19 crisis when many countries competed for limited availability of basic medical and health materials and equipment, including Covid vaccines. There have not yet been any effective measures that address issues relating to export controls at the WTO until this day.[33]

32 Led by the US and supported by Japan and the EU. See Trebilcock, Howse, & Eliason, 2012: 526–527.

33 There has been, however, a series of reports by the WTO on Covid and world trade, see www.wto.org/english/tratop_e/covid19_e/covid_reports_e.htm (last accessed 31/5/22).

5.3. The Liberal Foundation Maintained

If the Uruguay Round has been revolutionary in expanding the scope of GATT/WTO, the approach to addressing substantive issues was conversative, and so, the liberal foundation of GATT/WTO thus remains intact.

First, although the so-called GATT 1994 is, legally speaking, a separate and different treaty from GATT 1947 (Art II:4 of the WTO Agreement), it is in fact the GATT 1947 as amended, clarified, and supplemented by the various decisions, protocols, codes of conduct, and further agreements on specific issues. These additional legal instruments are of a technical nature, and none fundamentally affects the underlying principles of the GATT 1947. Indeed, all GATT 1947 principles, decisions and procedures remain in force unless modified by the Uruguay Round of negotiations (Art XVI.1 of WTO Agreement). In other words, the theoretical foundation of the GATT 1994 remains the same, with its operation modified by the supplementary technical agreements adopted at different times.

Secondly, it is not only the theoretical foundation of GATT that remains unchanged, the GATT, its structure and approach, has also served as the model upon which the regulation of the newly introduced subject-matters, that is, GATS, TRIPS and TRIMS, is established. Thus, the underlying principles for all these new agreements are to ease market access and to liberalise trade, both of which are to be established on the basis of non-discrimination through the principles of most-favoured-nation treatment, national treatment, and other non-discriminatory principles. In fact, the GATT model is followed so rigidly that the MFN treatment was also adopted by TRIPS agreement (Art 4 of the TRIPS Agreement). This principle requires a WTO member to extend any preferential treatment accorded to Member A to all other members. Since MFN is not a specific treatment, this principle then means that, at least theoretically, if a member treats all others poorly in the protection of intellectual property, its practice would be lawful, although it is hardly what the TRIPS has intended nor is it the best way to protect intellectual property involved in trade.

Thirdly, certain concessions are made for developing countries, and this is especially true of GATS which, strictly speaking, is still a work-in-progress. However, such concessions are about allowing trade liberalisation by developing countries to be a more gradual and scheduled process without the need to immediately match trade liberalisation promised by developed countries.

Finally, the new dispute resolution mechanism under the WTO is clearly adjudication-oriented, with formalism as its foundation and the removal of trade barriers as its objectives. As will be discussed in Chapter 5, although this approach soon found its challenges when the purview of the WTO further extended and membership expanded, the debate continues to be the same: how might the dispute resolution mechanism facilitate and foster freer trade?

In short, despite the significant expansion of the regulatory scope of GATT/WTO, the underlying (liberal) regulatory philosophy remains the same: freer trade on equal footing for all members.

6. Conclusion

The previous review of the development of the GATT/WTO suggests that the foundation of the GATT/WTO is the liberal market ideology that pursues freer trade. However, at the same time, the GATT/WTO was never meant to be a static system; it evolved through time, both in terms of depth and scope. At a practical level, the need to adjust tariffs periodically and to harness the various non-tariff measures, the improper use of which would impede free trade and undermine the liberal economic order, means that the gradual evolution of the GATT/WTO regulatory regime is practically inbuilt. Further, not only is the GATT/WTO regime an evolving system, the dynamics propelling its changes also evolves. While much of the changes during the GATT period was propelled by the need to reduce tariffs and to improve regulatory aspects within the ambit of GATT 'jurisdiction', the Kennedy Round (1962–7) began to see external pressures upon the GATT to address not only free trade but also fair trade, that is, to provide a better deal for developing countries.

Importantly, however, the membership of contracting parties has gradually expanded, and with it, the inclusion of more diversified economic systems and uneven economic development levels exist among the membership of GATT/WTO. This expansion and change of membership inevitably create difficulties and problems for less-developed countries under the principle of equality and non-discrimination to implement the rules whose foundation is built upon liberalism. It also demands better solutions for developing countries as well as accommodations for countries adhering to different economic systems. In other words, the seeds for contention had already been sown from the very beginning of the life of GATT, for the notions of 'fair' trade that were to emerge soon after the establishment of the GATT and 'fair' trade and less rigid application of the regulatory regimes requires differentiated treatment for members at different levels of development and/or with different politico-economic systems.

Equally important, as pointed out by Ruggie,

> the strength of these regimes, of course, is backed by the capabilities of the hegemon. If and as such a concentration of economic capabilities

> erodes, the liberal order is expected to unravel and its regimes to become weaker, ultimately being replaced by mercantilist arrangements, that is, by arrangements under which the constituent units reassert national political authority over transnational economic forces.
>
> (Ruggie, 1982: 381)

Indeed, with various new economic powers emerging since 1947, the world was soon to become multi-polar, and the Western domination was to be under increasing challenges throughout the period of GATT's existence, but especially after the establishment of the WTO which does not only have a larger membership but a much wider scope of trade regulation. These new powers soon began to assert certain powers in policy directions. This is especially so since the rise of China and, to a lesser degree, India. The ever-diversified membership, coupled with an ever-increasing scope of trade regulation, inevitably led to the formation of groups with shared interests, both within the GATT/WTO and outside it, and the latter means some major development of regional trade agreements. In the case of China, which is both a most powerful trading nation and a radically different politico-economic entity from the original hegemonic powers, such a regional development is eventually conflated to become a geopolitical and trading matter of contention between China and Western powers: an ugly struggle that continues today.

In short, three most important developments – preferential treatment for developing countries, regional agreements, and the rise of China (and the consequent geopolitical contention), each of which is a subject-matter for the following chapters – significantly challenges the liberal foundation of GATT/WTO, especially its core principle of non-discrimination and the faithful compliance with the GATT/WTO rules. The dynamic for change is, in its essence, a fusion of power and legitimate social purpose (Ruggie, 1982: 285), and such changes may or may not challenge the principles and the normative framework therein (Ruggie, 1982: 284). But, for the time being, as will be discussed in the following chapters, the liberal market ideology remains largely the foundation of this dynamic international trade regulatory regime, even though it has been increasingly threatened by both international geopolitical struggles and domestic socioeconomic trends (Mazarr et al., 2017).

References

Amadi, Luke (2020), 'Globalization and the changing liberal international order: A review of the literature', 2 *Research in Globalization*, available at www.sciencedirect.com/science/article/pii/S2590051X20300046?via%3Dihub (last accessed 24/10/21).

Awuku, Emmanual Opoku (1994), 'How do the results of the Uruguay round affect the North-South trade?' 2 (28) *Journal of World Trade* 73.

Cheeseman, Henry R. (1992), *Business Law: The Legal, Ethical and International Environment* (Englewood Cliffs, NJ: Prentice-Hall Inc).

Cohen, Harlan Grant (2019), 'What is international trade law for?' 113 (2) *The American Journal of International Law* 326.

DFAT (undated), 'Doha round', available at www.dfat.gov.au/trade/organisations/wto/Pages/doha-round (last accessed 11/10/21).

EC (1994), *The Uruguay Round: Global Agreement, Global Benefits* (Luxembourg: Official Publications of the EC).

GATT (1954), 'GATT: The ninth session of the contracting parties and the review of the GATT, 25 October 1954', available at https://docs.wto.org/gattdocs/q/GG/MGT/54-27.PDF (last accessed 12/10/21).

Islam, Rafiaqul (1993), 'GATT with emphasis on its dispute resolution system', in O. Wilde & R. Islamn (eds.), *International Transactions: Trade and Investment, Law and Finance* (Sydney: LBC).

Islam, Rafiqul (1999), *International Trade Law* (Sydney: LBC).

Jackson, John H. (1989), *The World Trading System: Law and Policy of International Economic Relations* (Cambridge, MA: The MIT Press).

Jahn, Beat (2018), 'Liberal internationalism: Historical trajectory and current prospects', 94 (1) *International Affairs* 43.

Keohane, Robert O. (1980), 'The theory of hegemonic stability and changes in international economic regimes, 1967–1977,' in Ole Holsti et al. (eds.), *Change in the International System* (Boulder, CO: Westview Press).

Kindleberger, Charles P. (1973), *The World in Depression, 1929–1939* (Berkeley: University of California Press).

Kohona, Palitha T. B. (1994), 'Dispute resolution under the word trade organisation', 28 (2) *Journal of World Trade* 23.

Mazarr, Michael J., Cevallos, Astrid Stuth, Priebe, Miranda, Radin, Andrew, Reedy, Kathleen, Rothenberg, Alexander D., Thompson, Julia A. & Willcox, Jordan (2017), *Measuring the Health of the Liberal International Order* (Santa Monica, CA: RAND Corporation).

McGovern, Edmond (1986), *International Trade Regulation: GATT, the United States and European Community* (Exeter: Globefield Press).

Rom, Michael (1994), 'Some early reflections on the Uruguay round agreement as seen from the viewpoint of a developing country', 28 (6) *Journal of World Trade* 5.

Ruggie, John Gerard (1982), 'International regimes, transactions, and change: embedded liberalism in the postwar economic order', (Spring) 36 (2) *International Organization* 379.

Sarcevic, Petar (1990), 'Impact of the international monetary system on world trade', in P. Sarcevic & H. van Houtte (eds.), *Legal Issues in International Trade* (London/Dordrecht/Boston: Graham & Trotman/Martinus Nijohff), 207–219.

Schill, Stephan W. (2014), '*Lex mercatoria*', in *The Max Planck Encyclopedia of Public International Law*, available at https://opil.ouplaw.com/view/10.1093/law:epil/9780199231690/law-9780199231690-e1534 (last accessed 25/10/21).

Skubik, Daniel W. (1993), 'International economic institutions', in O. Wilde & R. Islamn (eds.), *International Transactions: Trade and Investment, Law and Finance* (Sydney: LBC).

Stewart, Terence P. (ed.) (1993), *The GATT Uruguay Round: A Negotiating History (1986–1992), Vol. I: Commentary* (Deventer/Boston: Kluwer Law and Taxation Publishers).

Symposium on TRIPS and TRIMS (1991), 'Symposium on TRIPS and TRIMS in the Uruguay round: Analytical and negotiating issues', available at https://deepblue.lib.umich.edu/bitstream/handle/2027.42/100994/ECON435.pdf?sequence=1 (last accessed 21/10/21).

Trebilcock, M. J., Howse, R. & Eliason, A. (2012), *The Regulation of International Trade*, 4th edition (London/New York: Routledge).

Wolff, Alan Wm (2019), 'The current state of the world trading system and its likely future', 18 September, available at www.lowyinstitute.org/publications/current-state-world-trading-system-and-its-likely-future (last accessed 28/9/21).

WTO Analytical Index, 'The WTO analytical index: Guide to WTO law and practice', which is available on the WTO website: www.wto.org/english/res_e/publications_e/ai17_e/ai17_e.htm (last accessed 7/10/21).

WTO GATT Years (undated), 'The GATT years: From Havana to Marrakesh', available at www.wto.org/english/thewto_e/whatis_e/tif_e/fact4_e.htm (last accessed 8/10/21).

WTO Tariffs (undated), 'Tariffs: More bindings and closer to zero', available at www.wto.org/english/thewto_e/whatis_e/tif_e/agrm2_e.htm (last accessed 25/10/21).

WTO 20 Years (undated), 'WTO, trade and tariffs: Trade grows as tariffs decline: 20 Years of the WTO', available at www.wto.org/english/thewto_e/20y_e/wto_20_brochure_e.pdf (last accessed 12/10/21).

2 Fairer Trade

Developing Countries and the NIEO

1. Introduction

When the GATT was signed in 1947, 11 out of the original 23 contracting parties were 'developing countries'.[1] This composition of membership soon changed, as many newly independent states began to emerge as a result of decolonisation that followed the end of World War II. Most of these countries were, and many still are, economically underdeveloped countries. As a result, there has been a steady increase of developing countries participating in GATT/WTO.[2] Today, about two-thirds of the WTO's 164 members have the status of 'developing countries.'[3]

The rapid decolonisation process in many parts of the world then effectively created, in addition to the East-West divide that initially dominated the UN in its early years, the North-South divide that has played a critical role in the call to take into consideration the special needs of developing countries and for new rules, or at least changes to existing rules, for international trade and global economic cooperation. This divide ultimately led to the call for a New International Economic Order (NIEO). The demand for an NIEO or the cry for a more equitable trading system then led to the insertion of Part IV into the GATT and, eventually, the development of a 'Special

1 Often referred to as the 'Less-Developed Countries' in the early period of the GATT. See 'Background Document, 1999: 5. The 23 original contracting parties were Australia, Belgium, *Brazil*, *Burma*, Canada, *Ceylon*, *Chile*, (the Republic of) *China*, *Cuba*, Czechoslovak, France, *India*, *Lebanon*, Luxembourg, Netherlands, New Zealand, Norway, *Pakistan*, Southern *Rhodesia*, *Syria*, South Africa, UK, and USA. Developing countries are indicated by italics.

2 There were 25, 68 and 76 developing countries taking part in the last three rounds of negotiations respectively (the Kennedy, Tokyo and Uruguay Rounds). See Background Document, 1999: 5.

3 See www.wto.org/english/thewto_e/whatis_e/tif_e/dev1_e.htm (last accessed 5/6/22).

DOI: 10.4324/9781003275510-3

and Differential Treatment' (S&D) system for developing countries in the GATT/WTO.[4] Essentially, the S&D treatment is to provide preferential treatment to developing countries as an exception to the non-discrimination principles, especially the MFN treatment, in the GATT/WTO system. It represented the first major challenge to fundamental principles underlying the GATT/WTO regulatory system. However, in its nature, the fight was not against free trade, but for fairer trade.

The fight for fairer trade is, however, far from over. This contest for fairer trade within the WTO is unlikely to abate, according to some commentators, until and unless the perceived or genuinely unjust or unfair treatment of developing countries is addressed and remedied, and its direction of pursuing the old trade 'liberalisation' is reversed:

> The WTO, as if possessed of some obscure religious belief, advocates the universal application of an ideology so narrow, so utterly orthodox, so partial, so devoid of rational justification, so totally deranged, that it imagines nothing else. It pursues the 'liberalisation' of everything because it can think of no other reason for its own existence. It makes rules that must, by definition, eventually apply to all peoples, regardless of their outlook. . . . It glorifies all forms of 'growth' in feigned ignorance of any cancerous mutations, including its own.
>
> (Ransom, 2001: 10)

It has even been suggested that the medium-term viability of the WTO depends on an effective mechanism that would properly accommodate the needs of the 'developing countries' (Hoekman, 2003; Keck & Low, 2004). Yet, as pointed out by some major reports on WTO reform, developing countries' status remains a 'thorny and structural problem' for the WTO (Schneider-Petsinger, 2020: 32; also The Sutherland Report, 2004; The Warwick Report, 2008).

This chapter will review the movement towards fairer trade in recognition of different trading capacities of nations and in response to the special needs of developing countries. It will examine the S&D system that has been developed since 1964 and its actual effect as a first major challenge to the ideological foundation of the GATT/WTO regime.

4 Often referred to as 'special and more favourable' treatment under GATT before 1995 when the WTO was established. It should be noted that the original GATT (Art XVIII:1) contains such provisions only for those economies that 'support low standards of living and are in the early stages of development'.

2. Developing Countries in Context

The notion of 'developing countries' is frequently invoked in discussion and debate in international law, international trade, international relations and, of course, international politics; its meaning is, however, assumed and has never been precisely defined in the history of the UN or the GATT/WTO, though not without efforts to do so (Keck & Low, 2004: 10). The presumption that the notion of 'developing countries' has some agreed meanings is therefore false. If anything, it means different things in different contexts.

Initially, and largely in the context of the United Nations, hence, in the context of world politics, less developed countries were closely related to the notion of 'third world' – a phrase that was initially coined in the 1950s by the French anthropologist and historian Alfred Sauvy but widely used in the UN and world politics in the Cold War period – referring to those countries neither belonged to the NATO capitalist countries nor the socialist bloc but largely economically under-developed countries (Muni, 1979; Smit, 2013). The notion of 'third world' was replaced by the notion of 'developing countries' after the end of the Cold War.

Not only is the notion of 'developing countries' un-defined, the UN in fact uses the term rather loosely and sometimes other terms are used for different purposes. The United Nations Development Program (UNDP) classifies, for example, all countries other than the US, Europe, Canada, Australia, New Zealand and Japan as 'developing countries' (Trebilcock & Howse, 1999: 574). The World Bank (technically part of the UN), on the other hand, classifies countries on the basis of per capita Gross National Income and divides countries into low-income, lower-middle income, upper-middle income, and high-income countries.[5] Since 1971, the UN has recognised a new category of membership, that is, the Least Developed Countries (LDCs). The status of belonging to the LDCs is reviewed every three years by the United Nations Economic and Social Council in accordance with its three criteria: gross national income per capita, indicators of nutrition, health, school enrolment and literacy (human assets), and indicators of natural and trade-related shocks, physical and economic exposure to shocks, and smallness and remoteness (economic vulnerability).[6]

5 For 2021–2022 classification, see https://blogs.worldbank.org/opendata/new-world-bank-country-classifications-income-level-2021-2022 (last accessed 5/6/22).

6 The latest (2021) list includes 46 LDCs, comprising around 880 million people, 12 percent of the world population, which account for less than 2 percent of world GDP and around 1 percent of world trade. See https://unctad.org/topic/least-developed-countries/recognition (last accessed 31/10/21).

For the purposes of the GATT/WTO membership, it is a matter of self-assertion and acceptance by other members, although some of the provisions of WTO agreements do attempt to provide some vague 'criteria' for enjoying certain 'S&D' treatment. The practice of self-declaration and acceptance by WTO members, and its result in the actual designation of 'developing countries', is seriously problematic. One has to be completely blind to think that the same set of preferential trading rules should be equally applicable and appropriate to, say China or Hong Kong and Congo or Sierra Leone, or many other African countries.[7]

Not surprisingly, the WTO has for some years made some further differentiation between developing countries in some of its agreements. Many WTO agreements now allow LDCs a more 'lenient' trading discipline and a longer period to adjust any inconsistent policies, or they are simply allowed a 'free ride'. However, WTO agreements have not been consistent in this regard. For instance, under the Agreement on Subsidies and Countervailing Measures, developing countries are divided into LDCs as designated by the UN, countries whose GNP *per capita* income is below US$1,000, and other developing countries (Art 27.2 and Annex VII). In other words, LDCs will graduate from this designation once their GNP *per capita* income reaches US$1,000, a graduation criterion that excludes other factors set out by the UN. And more often than not, LDCs will have to compete with other 'developing countries' under the S&D treatment provisions.

In short, the notion of 'developing countries' is a messy and problematic one. While it encompasses countries at vastly different levels of socio-economic development and trading capacity there is only limited recognition of such differences by the UN and the WTO, with no consistent nor coherent approach. The definitional problems are, in fact, deeply rooted in the political context in which the notion initially emerged and was introduced into the GATT. This political context, to be discussed later, is critical in understanding developing countries as a force for changes at the WTO.

7 Not surprisingly, the US and EU declared, as early as in 1996, that such countries/regions as Hong Kong, Singapore, South Korea and China should be considered as 'developed countries', at least for the purpose of compliance with TRIPs. See Matsushita, Schoenbaum, Mavroidis, & Hahn, 2015: 704. Under pressure from Western countries, Brazil, South Korea, Singapore, and Taiwan announced in 2019 that they would no longer seek the special and differential treatment reserved for developing countries at the WTO. See Schneider-Petsinger, 2020: 33–35. On the other hand, Hong Kong has not done so, and China has declared that it would never relinquish its developing country status, but would relinquish many benefits for developing countries but retaining such a status in the WTO. See Farge, 2021.

3. The NIEO and Early Challenges to GATT Foundational Principles

As alluded to in Chapter 1, the United Nations, though principally responsible for world peace and security, was also established for the purpose of economic cooperation. Despite the fact that the GATT/WTO eventually developed outside the UN system, the 'twin' consideration in the establishment of the UN inevitably led to the convergence or, more precisely, confusion between a political right and an economic/trading right in the UN's efforts to establish an NIEO.

As previously discussed in Chapter 1, when the GATT was signed in 1947, the world was dominated by the US-led Western powers, politically and economically. The geo-political scene however began to change at the UN in the 1960s as a result of the UN-led decolonisation process in the 1960s which led to the independence of many countries from their former colonial powers, most of them being economically poor countries (or, as they were often referred to at the time Third World countries). By their voting strength on the principle of one-nation one-vote practiced in most world-wide organisations, these newly independent countries started to play a role in international relations, at least at the UN level, and significantly changed the geopolitical landscape of world politics. At the same time, the deterioration of the North-South economic gap after a decade of the so-called export-led development strategy became clear and was blamed on the 'old' international economic order established and controlled by Western industrialised countries (Trebilcock & Howse, 1999: 367–368). Not surprisingly, developing countries, supported by socialist countries, began to demand the establishment of an NIEO in the form of establishing new rules or at least making changes to existing rules on international economic relationships as well as the establishment of new inter-governmental institutions (Dell, 1985: 10–32).

The first success of this NIEO movement was the proclamation of a Development Decade by the General Assembly of the UN in 1961, which also had the support of the US and other Western countries. Further, and despite resistance from some developed countries, the famous Resolution 1803 was adopted on 14 December 1962, granting developing countries the right to nationalise foreign holdings so as to reduce foreign control over their economics, provided that they offer compensation according to international law.[8] The resolution and its implementation did not, however, fulfil

8 UN General Assembly Resolution 1803 (XVII): Permanent Sovereignty over Natural Resources, UN Document A/Res/1803 (XVII) 19 December 1962.

the expectations of the developing countries. Instead, the gap between them and the industrialised countries continued to increase despite efforts to the contrary (Dell, 1985: 14; Dicke, 1990: 23–24).

Efforts continued towards the goal of establishing an NIEO, especially pushed by the newly emerged group of non-aligned developing countries.[9] With their sheer majority at the UN General Assembly, they managed to secure the adoption of several UN Resolutions: in May 1974, the General Assembly adopted a Declaration and Programme of Action on the Establishment of a NIEO (Resolutions 3201 (S-VI) and 3202 (S-VI)), and in December of the same year, the Charter of the Economic Rights and Duties of States (Resolution 3281 (XXIX)). These documents proclaim some 20 principles on which the new economic order should be founded, i.e., the broadest co-operation of all States in fighting inequality, better prices for raw materials and primary commodities, active assistance to developing countries free of political conditions, the use of a reformed international monetary system for the better promotion of development and so on (Robertson & Merrills, 1996: 256–257). Significant as it may have been, and though supported by no less than 120 countries, the Charter was opposed by six of the developed countries,[10] with another 10 abstaining,[11] the majority of them being major international donors. As a result, the Charter remains a piece of paper of academic interest with little practical value (Dicke, 1990: 24).[12]

By 1964, and initially on the basis of *ad hoc* alliances among developing countries, the United Nations Conference on Trade and Development (UNCTAD) emerged as an 'institutional response in the economic sphere to the entry of the Third World on the international scene' (Cutajar, 1985: vii). From its very beginning, the governments that established the UNCTAD accepted a commitment 'to lay the foundations of a better world economic order' (Dell, 1985: 10), so as to directly tackle issues of inequality, worsening trade terms, and international capital flow (Dell, 1985: 10–32;

9 The group of non-aligned countries (Group-77) was first established at Bandung in 1955 with 77 members. Its membership has now nearly doubled.

10 Belgium, Denmark, the Federal Republic of Germany, Luxembourg, Great Britain and the USA.

11 Austria, Canada, France, Ireland, Israel, Italy, Japan, the Netherlands, Norway and Spain.

12 This however does not mean that there has been no impact of the notion of an NIEO upon international economic relations. One of the major concerns in trade and investment is the issue of national sovereignty over natural resources and economic activities (including foreign investment) and, consequently, the possibility of nationalisation. This led to the practice of bilateral agreements for the protection of investment as a result of the absence of a multilateral agreement (see Sornarajah, 1993: 310–333).

UNCTAD, 1985; Williams, 1991). It was at the first UNCTAD in 1964 that the North-South divide began to obscure the East-West conflict and render it to a secondary place within the framework of the UN (Williams, 1991: 43), and the North-South divide has remained the major focus of UNCTAD since.

Although UNCTAD is constitutionally required to act as a coordinating centre in the UN system in respect of international development policies (Williams, 1991: 57–58), it has no formal rule-making powers nor many specific implementation measures, nor is it particularly liked by developed countries which were and are still content with the Bretton Woods system as the principal force for global management of international economic relations. Not surprisingly, only relatively few of the UNCTAD's initiatives have led to practical results (Seidi-Hohenveldem, 1992: 95), among which are the insertion of Part IV into the GATT in 1964,[13] and the establishment of a Committee on Trade and Development in the same year to oversee the implementation of Part IV as well as the International Trade Centre (now a joint agency of UNCTAD and WTO) to promote the trade of developing countries (Background Document, 1999: 5).

The insertion of a new part into the GATT thus began the so-called 'S&D' treatment for developing countries, initially under the GATT but now further entrenched into the WTO agreements.

4. GATT/WTO Approach to and Mechanisms for Developing Countries

4.1. Towards a Differential and More Favourable Treatment

It should be pointed out, at the outset, that the original GATT was basically silent on the issue of developing countries as the notion itself and the North-South divide were yet to emerge. Indeed, and in strong contrast with the Agreement Establishing the WTO, the preamble of the GATT 1947 did not mention the words 'developing countries' at all. It was only after the first review session of the GATT (1954–1955) that GATT allowed countries 'the economies of which can only support low standards of living and are in the early stages of development' some flexibility to modify or withdraw

13 It should be pointed out that, prior to the adoption of Part IV, GATT had adopted a number of decisions and measures that were designed to support the less-developed countries (as they were then called). Other concessions were further obtained by developing countries in the 1970s. The effect of Part IV and later concessions is to waive certain GATT requirements in favour of developing countries (see Background Document, 1999; Seidi-Hohenveldem, 1992: 90).

their tariff concessions and to permit some limited measures to protect a particular industry or balance-of-payments under Art XVIII.[14] Although Annex I to the GATT attempts to provide some elaboration, no specific criteria have been established for determining which countries would be qualified as such 'economies'. Nevertheless, an economy supporting low standards of living is only to be judged on the basis of 'the normal condition of that economy' and an economy in the early stages of development would also include a country undergoing a process of industrialisation to diversify away from an excessive dependence on primary production (Annex I: *Ad Art XVIII)*.

The Provisions in Part IV of GATT are, as has frequently been pointed out, remarkably vague and fundamentally inspirational in approach,[15] although, like Art XVIII of the GATT, they explicitly allow some differential treatment for developing countries (still called less-developed countries). Nevertheless, these provisions kick-started the movement and maintained a momentum for special treatment to be accorded to developing countries. In particular, UNCTAD continued to call for 'unanimous agreement in favour of the early establishment of a mutually acceptable system of generalised, non-reciprocal and non-discriminatory preferences which would be beneficial to the developing countries' in the mid-1960s (Background Document, 1999: 15). This then led to the development of some special treatment typically represented by the so-called 'Generalised System of Preference' (GSP)[16] and the 'Enabling Clause'[17] which later institutionalised the GSP in GATT/WTO.

The GSP, initially promoted by UNCTAD, was developed in a variety of international institutions, and finally adopted in 1971 by GATT for a ten-year period as a waiver to MFN (most-favoured-nation status).[18] The waiver authorises each industrialised country to establish its own GSP program

14 Initially entitled 'Government assistance to economic development and reconstruction' (now 'Government assistance to economic development') and intended to provide some flexibility to all countries (Background Documents, 1999: 5).

15 WTO defines such as being in the nature of guidelines (see Background Document, 1999: 5).

16 Under the Generalized System of Preferences, developed countries offer non-reciprocal preferential treatment (such as zero or low duties on imports) to products originating in developing countries.

17 A Decision adopted at the 1979 Tokyo Round, entitled 'Decision on Differential and More Favourable Treatment, Reciprocity and Fuller Participation of Developing Countries'.

18 There were, at least initially, disputes as to whether Part IV of the GATT would allow a generalised system of preference without undermining the general principles of GATT (e.g., MFN, etc.) (see Background Document, 1999: 5; Jackson, 1997: 321–322).

without the need to accord the same to other Contracting Parties under the MFN principle. However, it was left to each industrialised country, in the absence of any specific guidelines, to define what a 'developing country' was for purposes of benefiting from the GSP program. The result is that each country has its own GSP practice and has introduced their practice at different times (the US being the last, in 1974, to implement GSP through its Trade Act 1974).[19]

More specific measures were to be worked out during the 1979 Tokyo Round, which was mandated to 'secure additional benefits for the international trade of developing countries' in the recognition of 'the importance of the application of differential measures to developing countries in ways which will provide special and more favourable treatment for them in areas of the negotiations where this is feasible and appropriate' (Background Document, 1999: 15). Hence, a number of codes adopted at the 1979 Tokyo Round have special provisions for developing countries.[20] Importantly, the previous mentioned 'Enabling Clause' was adopted at this Round of negotiations.

In relation to the previous development, it is important to note that, first, such concessions and allowances were made under pressure from developing countries aspiring to establish a NIEO or at least to rectify some of the problems with the 'old' order. Secondly, although 'developing countries' as a group began to acquire some legal consequences under GATT rules, LDCs as a notion also began to emerge and gain importance in the GATT system. Finally, although favourable treatment was provided to developing countries, items important for the promotion of their export-led growth, such as textiles, light manufactures and processed agricultural products encountered very high trade barriers in developed countries (Trebilcock & Howse, 1999: 302). At the same time, the so-called 'grey-area measures', such as 'voluntary export restraints (VERs) or 'orderly marketing arrangements' (OMAs) were also devised by developed countries with some particularly severe effects on developing countries (Background Document, 1999). Thus, the practical benefits of such S&D treatment are clearly questionable.

19 Such a decision is now made by the US President (Jackson, 1997: 324). In the EC, GSP is implemented through the Lomé Convention (now Lomé IV), which grants some 65 developing countries (almost all of them are ex-colonies of UK and/or France) (see Trebilcock & Howse, 1999: 373).

20 For instance, the Agreement on Technical Barriers to Trade, Art XII; the Agreement on Government Procurement, Art III; the Subsidies Code, Part III Art 14; and the Antidumping Code, Art 14.

4.2. Back to Non-discrimination & Liberalisation

One aspect of the Uruguay Round negotiations (1986–1994) that is often forgotten is the negotiation mandate in relation to improvement of trading treatment for developing countries.[21] Thus, several general principles governing negotiations as set down by the Ministerial Declaration on the Uruguay Round specifically required special attention to be given to developing countries, including non-reciprocal treatment and measures to facilitate expansion of their trading opportunities.[22]

The reality of the Uruguay Round was that the main negotiations were conducted among the developed countries themselves, esp. the three main powers, Japan, US and EU, and only extended to the developing countries on an MFN basis (Rom, 1994: 6). More importantly, GATT principles concerning developing countries only managed to be mentioned in an *ad hoc* fashion in various documents providing a few concessions for developing countries.[23] This implies that the previously mentioned negotiation principles are no longer, in the language of one commentator, the 'explicit right of the developing countries (other than the least developed countries) and that it is open to the discretion of the developed countries, if they so desire, to exert pressure to obtain more commitments and concessions than are actually justified' (Rom, 1994: 8).

The only special decision taken at the Uruguay Round was about the LDCs: [Ministerial] Decision on Measures in Favour of Least-Developed Countries. This Decision reaffirmed the commitment contained in the 'Enabling Clause' but is apparently only applicable to LDCs. It was decided that, 'if not already provided for in the instruments negotiated in the course of the Uruguay Round, notwithstanding their acceptance of these instruments, the least-developed countries, and for so long as they remain in that category, while complying with the general rules set out in the aforesaid instruments, will only be required to undertake commitments and concessions to the extent consistent with their individual development, financial and trade needs, or their administrative and institutional capabilities.' (Item 1 of the Decision). Other agreements in the Decision are phrased in very general terms which are, as usual, merely aspirational.

21 Thus, it was meant to be a great 'North-South bargain' (see North-South Institute, 2003: 1).

22 See the general principles for the Uruguay Negotiations Items (4)-(7), available at https://docs.wto.org/gattdocs/q/GG/GATTFOCUS/41.pdf (5/6/22).

23 e.g., Agreement on Technical Barriers; on Subsidies and Countervailing Measures (see Trebilcock & Howse, 1999: ch.14). Although pre-Uruguay GATT agreements and decisions are part of the WTO package, the applicability of GATT principles (including the 'Enabling Clause') to areas other than trade in goods is questioned by some scholars (see Rom, 1994: 7).

The previous also needs to be understood in the context that the Uruguay Round included, as discussed in Chapter 1, the introduction of new subject matters for the WTO, namely the GATS, TRIPs and TRIMs, none of which is of great benefit to less developed countries. It was no secret that developing countries only agreed to include these issues either because certain concessions were made to them by developed countries, or through fear of being left out or simply because they had little choice but to accept (Rom, 1994: 8–9; Awuku, 1994). In this context, the concessions made by developing countries can only be described as tremendous and as amounting to a major set-back in securing their national interests in global trade.

The end results of Uruguay thus represent:

> a change of heart and attitude from the more developed countries, returning to the basic rules of the original GATT, favouring non-discrimination and liberalisation as the fundamental tenets of the international trading system for all to be generally applicable with the minimum number of exceptions possible, the basic philosophy being that liberalisation, competition, non-intervention by government and non-discrimination are the best medicine for all – disregarding the specific circumstances and conditions in the Member countries.
>
> (Rom, 1994: 7)

It should, however, be pointed out that, during the Uruguay Round negotiations (especially the final days), developing countries had been reduced to being 'spectators on the side-lines' (Awuku, 1994: 92). Some larger developing countries nevertheless contributed to the less than desirable results as they had a change of heart, believing they could achieve more individually from developed countries through concrete bilateral agreements (Rom, 1994: 8).

5. A Failed Challenge

As of March 2021, there were now some 155 S&D provisions (WTO S&D Provisions, 2021). These provisions, according to the WTO, are to serve the developing countries by way of:

- increasing the trade opportunities for developing country members;
- safeguarding the interests of developing country members;
- allowing flexibility of commitments, of action, and use of policy instruments;
- granting transitional time-periods;
- providing technical assistance; and
- offering concessions to members that are LDCs.

On paper, the list looks impressive and, on this basis, developing countries can easily claim a political victory. However, as trading rights, the success must be assessed by tangible criteria, that is, their enforceability and the actual effectiveness in assisting developing countries in their pursuit of development through trade.

First, the S&D treatment accorded to developing countries under GATT first emerged in a more political than trading context, and was seen, and still is largely seen, as a political right (Keck & Low, 2004: 4). As such, the S&D provisions are remarkably vague and fundamentally inspirational in approach,[24] technically referred to as the 'best endeavour' provisions, and legally described as 'non-mandatory and unenforceable' (IISD, 2003: 1; Keck & Low, 2004: 4). Although, like Art XVIII of the GATT, they explicitly allow some differential and preferential treatment for developing countries as exceptions; they were never meant to challenge the liberal economic order that the GATT/WTO is meant to maintain.

Secondly, as just mentioned previously, the Uruguay Round negotiations re-affirmed liberalism as the foundation of WTO, with its fundamental objectives being the liberalisation of trade through reducing trade barriers and non-discrimination. Not surprisingly, other than provisions on longer transitional periods as contained in individual agreements, few of the S&D provisions are specific or legally enforceable. At the same time, the movement towards liberalisation, competition, and non-discrimination as the fundamental underlying principles of the WTO trading regime is unmistakeable (Rom, 1994: 7). None of the new subject matters such the GATS, TRIPs, TRIMs is of great benefit to less developed countries other than some large developing countries such as China and India (Sornarajah, 2004: 224–250). It is simply irrational to emphasise trade liberalisation, competition and non-discrimination while trying to provide differentiated treatment in the rules without clear qualifications.

Thirdly, one must not see the GATT/WTO in isolation from the other two important pillars of the Bretton Woods system, namely the World Bank and IMF, both of which practise a weighted vote system and are hence constitutionally controlled by the rich nations.[25] Although the weighted vote system is absent from the GATT/WTO, as a matter of practice, GATT/WTO generally avoided formal voting, preferring a 'consensus' approach. It is, however, no secret that negotiations had been, before the rise of China and

24 As previously mentioned, WTO defines such as being in the nature of guidelines. See Background Document, 1999: 5.

25 The weighted vote system simply means that the value of a vote of each member is in proportion to the actual monetary contribution to the Bank/Fund.

India, conducted among and between the three powers (US, EU, and Japan, but sometimes with Canada as the fourth power, often referred to as the Quad) which effectively set the agenda and trading policy and rules for GATT/WTO. This is especially so as only the large developing countries participated actively in the core business of the GATT/WTO in negotiating market access exchange.

Finally, the post-Uruguay development suggests that the S&D provisions are to remain fundamentally political aspirations. Indeed, it did not take long for developing countries to realise that the trade-off or compromise they had made during the Uruguay Round was not a win-win result. They soon demanded a new 'development' round and, after the spectacular failure to produce results at Seattle, a new development round – the Doha Round – was indeed launched in November 2001. As a 'Development Round', Para. 44 of the Doha Ministerial Declaration (2001) called for a review of all S&D provisions 'with a view to strengthening them and making them more precise, effective and operational'. Para 12 of the Decision on Implementation-Related Issues and Concerns (2001) instructed the Committee on Trade and Development to 'identify those special and differential treatment provisions that are already mandatory in nature and those that are non-binding in character, to consider the legal and practical implications for developed and developing Members of converting special and differential treatment measures into mandatory provisions, to identify those that Members consider should be made mandatory, and to report to the General Council with clear recommendations for a decision' and to 'examine additional ways in which special and differential treatment provisions can be made more effective, to consider ways, including improved information flows, in which developing countries, in particular the least-developed countries, . . . and to report to the General Council with clear recommendations for a decision . . .'. These tasks were to be completed by July 2002, and the deadline was later extended a number of times, but the Committee repeatedly failed to complete its mandated tasks because 'differences among Members on the best way to proceed could not be bridged.'[26] Ultimately, little was achieved before 2015 when Members failed to reach a consensus on continuing multilateral trade negotiations.

In fact, the failure at the Doha Round is almost pre-determined by the inherently contradictory demands by developing countries. For instance, at the Hong Kong Conference, the Indian Minister of Commerce pointed out that 'our problems and challenges are so manifold and our socio-economic contexts so diverse, that no single, 'harmonised' development strategy can

26 See Report to the General Council by the Chairman of the Special Session of the Committee on Trade and Development, 29 July 2005, TN/CTD/13.

be adopted. Each country must choose the path that best suits its own genius' (Nath, 2005). If this is so, one wonders how the WTO could work out a one-size-for-all S&D for all developing countries. Further, while China, India and many other developing countries have strongly resisted the creation of any sub-classification of developing countries (Suryanarayana, 2005), LDCs are now firmly a sub-classification. Other sub-categories, such as 'Small Economies', 'Recently-acceded Members', have also appeared in WTO programs and declarations, many of them creations by developing countries themselves.[27] Thus, it is simply irrational to provide a one-size development strategy to a greatly diversified group of members.

Fundamentally, the S&D notion does not sit comfortably with the underlying philosophy of free trade embodied in the GATT/WTO. Indeed, despite the failure of the development agenda at Doha Round, the very small progress made at the Hong Kong conference was described by a long-term observer of the WTO, Alan Oxley, as 'a further dumbing down of the world body's free-market mission'.[28] In short and for all intents and purposes, the first ever challenge made to the underlying principles of the GATT/WTO has so far failed, and there is little evidence to suggest that such a failure will be reversed any time soon.

6. Fairer Trade: Between a Political Right and a Trading Rule

After a detailed examination of S&D provisions, Keck and Low reached the following conclusion:

> In sum, the vast majority of S&D provisions are somewhat blunt policy instruments in that they do not distinguish among developing country Members in terms of their differing development needs, access to some S&D provisions is left to the discretion of the WTO membership as a whole, and most provisions define beneficiaries in terms of an ill-specified group called developing countries.
>
> (Keck & Low, 2004: 24)

27 Informally, of course, there are such groups as ACP (African, Caribbean and Pacific Countries, also referred to as G-77 but consists of 56 members), African Group (41 countries), FANs (Friends of Antidumping Negotiations, 11 members), FIPs (or the Five or the Quint), G-10 (9 members), G-20 (21 members), G-33 (42 members) and G-90 (64 members), etc.

28 Oxley further described India's proposal that the WTO's rules on intellectual property be revised so law on industrial property will recognise the social values of pre-industrial society as laughable (Oxley, 2005).

Indeed, any well-intended effort to create 'fairer' trade for developing countries must face this reality: a political right is not the same as a trading rule, and in the latter case, it is unlikely that the dominating powers, that is, the developed nations and large developing countries, will accept any fundamental changes to the theoretical foundation of the GATT/WTO, that is, liberalisation of trade and equal competition. If this is the case, whatever the efforts that are being made for a 'fairer' trade could only be exceptions to the liberal economic order, not replacements of it. However, if S&D provisions are exceptions to the underlying principles of the GATT/WTO regulatory regime, they could not conceptually be made available to two thirds of the membership. Technically, it also means that coherence and integrity of the WTO regulatory regime must be maintained, and to do so, exceptions could only be made to a small number of members and such members cannot be self-proclaimed. Integrity also means enforceability of rules, not just 'rights' that are aspirational, admirable but ineffective. As they stand now, the notion of 'developing countries' is politically charged and the S&D provisions are operationally ineffective.

The lesson here is, while it is easy to introduce a political right into a trade regulatory regime, the translation of such a political right into a trading rule will face tremendous difficulties. This is especially so when a 'one-size-fits-all' principle and an 'open, export-oriented' approach are taken in a world where not all countries have a comparative advantage in trade (see also Thomas, 2003), nor free market and an open economy is necessarily the only model for development available or worth pursuing, as many economists would like us to believe (Balakrishnan, 2003: 3166–3167). Indeed, 'it appears that in the early 21st century it is the least globalised countries that are the best performers' (Balakrishnan, 2003: 3169).

Even under the comparative advantage theory, it has been pointed out that certain advantages (endowments) are more difficult to create than others (e.g., human capital) and some almost impossible to change (land ratio per capita), and thus the development path of East Asia simply will not fit the situation of Africa (Bonaglia & Fukasaku, 2003: 12). The economic development in South East Asia, China and India was not propelled by liberalisation of trade, but, on the contrary, it was the protected development that later led to trade (Balakrishnan, 2003: 3169; Thomas, 2003: 1405). In fact, in the past no countries have liberalised trade before their development: not the US, Britain, Germany, Japan or Taiwan (Elliott, 2003: 11). Common sense would also dictate that unless an economy has a sizeable market (which, comparatively, is always the case in developed countries) and it is developing at a reasonable rate, or unless the country is highly developed economically and technologically, there can be little need for trade nor indeed anything competitive to be offered for trade.[29] In fact, 'developing countries' have been locked in fierce competition for decades.

Despite its pro-development rhetoric, it is clear that S&D treatment offers very little practical value to countries that found difficulty in coping with the tide of globalisation and global trade. It is also clear that S&D fails to recognise the competing nature of relationships among developing countries. If it makes little sense to talk about developing countries as one group in terms of international trade; it makes no sense either to talk about general S&D treatment for all developing countries, not to mention the doubtful benefit of it for developing countries. Fundamentally, in international trade, it is the state and institutional capacity of a particular country in global competition that counts for the actual gaining of global trade benefits. In short, the S&D treatment, though initiated in the aspiration of a NIEO, has now become diverted into certain vague and non-binding concessions to trade liberalisation and, hence, has outlived its purpose. So far, much of the effort to reform in this area focuses on S&D treatment *per se*, with the ultimate goal of preserving the S&D provisions and making them more 'operational'.[30] These efforts have failed to address the much more deeply rooted problems in the S&D mechanism. In fact, conceptual confusion, political sensitivity, structural incoherence, and practical irrationality have led to the ineffectiveness of S&D provisions.

7. Conclusion

The demand for special treatment for developing countries is in fact part of a large challenge to the post-War liberal international order. It is strictly a sub-movement at the UN where the liberal idea of the human rights movement was assaulted by a vague notion of the Right to Development. That movement was extended to economic cooperation on the argument that a new economic order is 'an essential element for the effective promotion of human rights and fundamental freedoms', and then emphasised that the right to development is a human right and that equality of opportunity for

29 For detailed analyses of trade statistics and economic development, see Chen, 2004.

30 As mentioned previously, this is also true of the two current major reports (The Sutherland Report, 2004; The Warwick Report, 2008) on reforming the WTO despite the fact that both reports outline many problems in the S&D provisions and practice and its politicization (see also Hoekman, Michalopulos, & Winters, 2003: 3). More recently there have also been calls to move beyond S&D treatment by way of establishing plurilateral agreements, or creating specific development provisions for developing countries, or adopting a new 'development framework' in the WTO to determine the applicability of WTO disciplines to different countries (see Hoekman, 2005: 223–244).

development is as much a prerogative of nations as of individuals within nations.[31] That movement however failed, just like the challenge to the liberal economic order at the GATT/WTO (For further analysis, see Chen, 2008).

It is clear that a political right must not be confused with a trading rule, and an aspirational idea may not easily be translated into a binding and operational mechanism. In fact, such incorporation of a political right into a trade regulatory regime might cause more damage to trade than benefits and unnecessary complications for effective solutions to an identified problem, the problem of how to achieve fairer trade. It is important to keep in mind that WTO is a trading regulatory organisation which performs best when it focuses on its core functions. In this context, it is worthwhile keeping in mind the warning by Walden Bello, if the WTO fails to understand its own core functions, '[t]he WTO may eventually suffer the fate it helped inflict on the UNCTAD: surviving but increasingly ineffective and irrelevant' (Bello, 2003).

While it can be said that the first major challenge to the liberal foundation of the GATT/WTO has essentially failed, other challenges continue to emerge, with varied outcomes. In all, as will be discussed in the following chapters, the liberal foundation of the global trade regulatory regime proves to be stable, though not static, and capable of evolving to changing and changed geopolitical and economic circumstances.

References

Awuku, E. O. (1994), 'How do the results of the Uruguay round affect the North-South trade?' 28 (6) *Journal of World Trade* 75.

Background Document (1999), 'Background document to the high-level symposium on trade and development', Geneva, 17–18 March 1999, prepared by the Development Division of WTO, available at www.wto.org (last accessed 6/4/99).

Balakrishnan, P. (2003), 'Globalisation, growth and justice', (26 July 2003) *Economic and Political Weekly* 3166–3167.

Bello, Walden (2003), 'There is life after Cancún', *Bangkok Post*, 21 September, available at www.tni.org/archives/bello/cancun2.htm (last accessed 1/10/03).

Bonaglia, F. & Fukasaku, K. (2003), 'Export diversification in low-income countries: An international challenge after Doha', Technical Papers No. 209, OECD Development Centre, DEV/DOC, 7 June 2003, available at www.oecd.org/data oecd/13/28/8322001.pdf (last accessed 1/7/04).

31 See Resolution 32/130 (1977) and Resolution 34/46 (1979), both entitled 'Resolution on Alternative Approaches and Ways and Means within the United Nations System for Improving the Effective Enjoyment of Human Rights and Fundamental Freedoms'.

Chen, J. & Walker, G. (2004), *Balancing Act: Law Policy and Politics in Globalisation and Global Trade* (Sydney: Federation Press).

Chen, Jianfu (2008), 'Fairer trade & the human right to development – a perfect match or misconceived twin', *Forum on Public Policy Online*, Summer 2008 edition (January 2009), available at http://forumonpublicpolicy.com/summer08papers/papers08summer.html (last accessed 1/3/09).

Cutajar, M. Z. (1985), *UNCTAD and the South-North Dialogue: The First Twenty Years* (Oxford: Pergamon Press).

Dell, S. (1985), 'The origins of UNCTAD', in Cutajar (1985).

Dicke, D. C. (1990), 'Public international law and a new international economic order', in Sarcevic & van Houtte (1990).

Elliott, L. (2003), 'Free trade is fine in a world of equals', *The Guardian Weekly*, 11–17 September 2003.

Farge, Emma (2021), 'Envoy says China will forego many "developing country" benefits at WTO', 11 December, available at www.reuters.com/markets/commodities/exclusive-envoy-says-china-will-forego-many-developing-country-benefits-wto-2021–12–10/ (last accessed 11/12/21).

Hoekman, B. (2003), 'More favourable treatment of developing countries and the doha development agenda', *Trade Note*, 29 May, The World Bank. A PDF text is available from the World Bank website: http://www-wds.worldbank.org/servlet/WDS_IBank_Servlet?pcont=details&eid=000090341_20031010133 (last accessed 3/12/03).

Hoekman, B. (2005), 'Operationalising the concept of policy space in the WTO: Beyond special and differential treatment', in Petersmann (2005).

Hoekman, B., Michalopulos, C. & Winters, L. A. (2003), 'More favourable and differential treatment of developing countries: Toward a new approach in the World Trade Organisation', World Bank Policy Research Working Paper, WPS 3107. A PDF text is available form the World Bank website: http://www-wds.worldbank.org/servlet/WDS_IBank_Servlet?pcont=details&eid=000094946_03082104020550 (last accessed 7/7/03).

Hoekman, B. & Özden, C. (2005), 'Trade preferences and differential treatment of developing countries: A selective survey', World Bank Policy Research Working Paper 3566 (April 2005). A PDF text is available from the World Bank website: http://www-wds.worldbank.org/servlet/WDS_IBank_Servlet?pcont=details&eid=000012009_20050421124442 (last accessed 8/8/05).

IISD (2003), 'Special and differential treatment', 1 (13) *Doha Round Briefing Series*.

Jackson, J. H. (1997), *The World Trading System: Law and Policy of International Economic Relation*, 2nd edition (Cambridge, MA: The MIT Press).

Keck, A. & Low, P. (2004), 'Special and differential treatment in the WTO: Why, when and how', WTO Staff Working Paper ERSD-2004–03. A PDF text is available from the WTO website: www.wto.org/english/res_e/reser_e/ersd200403_e.htm (last accessed 1/08/05).

Matsushita, M., Schoenbaum, T. J., Mavroidis, P. C. & Hahn, M. (2015), *The World Trade Organisation: Law, Practice, and Policy*, 3rd edition (Oxford: Oxford University Press).

Moore, Mike (2003), *A World Without Walls: Freedom, Development, Free Trade and Global Governance* (Cambridge: Cambridge University Press).

Muni, S. D. (1979), 'The "third world" concept and controversy', (July) 1 (3) *Third World Quarterly* 119.

Nath, Kamal (2005), 'Statement at the sixth session of ministerial conference', 14 December, WT/MIN(05)/ST/17.

North-South Institute (2003), 'The reality of trade: The WTO and developing countries', available at www.nsi-ins.can/ensi/pdf/Reality_of_Trade.pdf (last accessed 1/5/04).

Oxley, Alan (2005), 'Anyone for global free trade deals?' *The Australian*, 19 December 2005, available at www.theaustralian.news.com.au/printpage/0,5942,17604 342,00.html (last accessed 20/12/05).

Petersmann, Ernst-Ulrich (ed.) (2005), *Reforming the World Trading System: Legitimacy, Efficiency, and Democratic Governance* (Clarendon: Oxford University Press).

Ransom, D. (2001), 'If the WTO means to stay afloat it will have to lose some excess baggage', 334 *New Internationalist* 9.

Robertson, A. H. & Merrills, J. G. (1996), *Human Rights in the World* (Manchester: Manchester University Press).

Rom, M. (1994), 'Some early reflections on the Uruguay round agreement as seen from the viewpoint of a developing country', 28 (6) *Journal of World Trade* 5.

Sarcevic, P. & van Houtte, H. (eds.) (1990), *Legal Issues in International Trade* (Dordrecht: Martinus Nijihoff).

Schneider-Petsinger, Marianne (2020), *Reforming the World Trade Organization Prospects for Transatlantic Cooperation and the Global Trade System* (London, September: Chatham House), available at www.chathamhouse.org/sites/default/files/publications/research/2020-09-11-reforming-wto-schneider-petsinger.pdf.pdf (last accessed 27/10/21).

Seidi-Hohenveldem, I (1992), *International Economic Law*, 2nd edition (Dordrecht: Matinus Nijhoff Publishers).

Smit, Nico (2013), 'The continued relevance of the "third world" concept', 26 March, available at www.e-ir.info/2013/03/26/the-continued-relevance-of-the-third-world-concept/ (last accessed 31/10/21).

Sornarajah, M. (1993), 'Bilateral investment treaties', in O. Wilde & R. Islamn (eds.), *International Transactions: Trade and Investment, Law and Finance* (Sydney: LBC).

Sornarajah, M. (2004), 'Good corporate citizenship and the conduct of multinational corporations', in Chen & Walker (2004), 224–250.

Suryanarayana, P. S. (2005), 'WTO: India, China oppose bid to divide developing countries', *The Hindu*, 13 July 2005, available at www.thehindu.com/2005.07/13/stories/2005071318661200.htm (last accessed 14/7/05).

The Sutherland Report (2004), 'The future of the WTO: Addressing institutional challenge in the new millennium', Report by the Consultative Board to the Director-General Supachai Panitchpakdi, The World Trade Organization.

Thomas, C. (2003), 'Poverty reduction, trade, and rights', 18 *American University International Law Review* 1399.

Trebilcock, M. J. & Howse, R. (1999), *The Regulation of International Trade*, 2nd edition (London/New York: Routledge).
UNDP (1999), 'Human development report', available at http://hdr.undp.org/reports/global/1999/en/ (last accessed 2/3/20).
The Warwick Report (2008), 'The multilateral trade regime: Which way forward?' The Report of the First Warwick Commission, The University of Warwick.
Williams, M. (1991), *Third World Cooperation: The Group of 77 in UNCTAD* (London: Printer Publishers).
WTO S&D Provisions (2021), 'Special and differential treatment provisions in WTO agreements and decisions', Note by the Secretariat, WT/COMTD/W/258, 2 March, available at https://docs.wto.org/dol2fe/Pages/SS/directdoc.aspx?filename=q:/WT/COMTD/W258.pdf&Open=True (last accessed 1/11/21).

3 Regional Trade Agreements

Complementary or Geopolitical

1. Introduction

Multilateral, regional and bilateral agreements and arrangements have co-existed in international trade law ever since, perhaps, the emergence of trade law. However, the inter-relationship among them and their relative weight in trade liberalisation have been in a constant state of flux, and each of them has often been controversial as to its nature as well as its relationship vis-à-vis the others.

On paper, concluding a regional trade agreement (RTA) does not violate GATT/WTO rules, and the existence of RTAs has often been described as being complementary to efforts for global trade liberalisation. However, at a time when the membership of the WTO already exceeds 160[1] and there are, at the same time, over 350 RTAs, some of which are described as super/mega-RTAs, and with their members being also, in the most part, members of the WTO, there is clearly a danger that the integrity and coherence of the WTO are being eroded. As will be discussed later, the expansion of the RTAs can be explained by various causes. However, the recent 'resurrection' of the ever-expanding regime of RTAs but especially the negotiation, and the conclusion of some of them, the 'super' RTAs – the TPP/CPTPP,[2] TTIP,[3] RCEP[4] and most recently the IPEF[5] – suggest the existence of a

1 The WTO membership reached 164 in July 2016 and it has been maintained at this level since then. See www.wto.org/english/thewto_e/whatis_e/tif_e/org6_e.htm (last accessed 23/4/22).

2 The Trans-Pacific Partnership/The Comprehensive and Progressive Agreement for Trans-Pacific Partnership (concluded).

3 The Transatlantic Trade and Investment Partnership (negotiations discontinued in April 2019).

4 The Regional Comprehensive Economic Partnership (concluded).

5 The Indo-Pacific Economic Framework for Prosperity (on-going).

DOI: 10.4324/9781003275510-4

geopolitical contest between existing and rising powers.[6] Even though the US withdrew from the TPP in 2017, there is little doubt that such negotiations amounted to a showdown between the existing powers (i.e., the US and the EU) and the emerging powers (especially China) for domination and primacy in the international economic order. In other words, this showdown is best understood in the context of the shifting balance of economic powers between the existing powers and the rising ones, and of the search for a new equilibrium in the international economic order. In this context, it is important to keep in mind the establishment of the Post-War international economic order, the challenges it has faced ever since its establishment, the stalemate at the Doha Round of negotiations, and the present geopolitical situation brought about by the long and continuing ascent of the emerging Asian powers, especially China.

This chapter first reviews, briefly, the development of RTAs beside the GATT/WTO, highlighting certain notable features of their development. It is then focused on the context in which the 'super' RTAs have emerged and been negotiated. It concludes that the rapid and substantive development of RTAs, often with a geopolitical approach, may well undermine the liberal economic order as the foundation of GATT/WTO, and significantly fracture the supposedly global regulatory regime as 'the only' regulatory regime and, as such, seriously undermine multilateralism.

2. GATT/WTO and RTAs

The original GATT – Art XXIV – allows for the formation and operation among contracting parties of customs unions, free trade areas and interim agreements leading to either of these arrangements to be made outside and alongside the GATT. Similarly, the GATS (Art V) under the WTO also made the allowance for the formation of additional arrangements outside the GATS. Additionally, agreements such as those that grant special benefits by developed nations to developing countries have further extended the application of the exception to WTO rules,[7] including the use of waiver under GATT/WTO.[8] These provisions, in their legal nature, make special exceptions to the non-discrimination principles under the GATT/WTO by

6 For a definition of rising powers, see Narlikar, 2013: 561–562: 'Rising powers are defined as those states that have established themselves as veto-players in the international system, but have still not acquired agenda-setting power'. See also Hart & Jones, 2010: 64–68.

7 See the 1979 Decision on Differential and More Favorable Treatment, Reciprocity and Fuller Participation of Developing Countries (the Enabling Clause).

8 See Art XXV of GATT and Understanding in Respect of Waiver of Obligations under the GATT 1994.

limiting preferential treatment among participating members of the relevant agreement. As such, they are often referred to as a preferential trade agreement (PTA).[9]

Although it is not clear what the particularly dominant reason for the creation of Art XXIV of the GATT was (Matsushita, Schoenbaum, Mavroidis, & Hahn, 2015: 508), it was nevertheless agreed that this article was designed for the purpose of trade creation, not trade diversion (Jackson, 1989: 141). It is also contested as to whether these provisions produce benefits or disadvantages or damages to the multilateral trade regime (that is, the GATT/WTO).[10] While restrictions are imposed by the application of Art XXIV and these restrictions were further elaborated, at the Uruguay Round, by the Understanding on the Interpretation of Art XXIV of the GATT 1994, this GATT article has effectively opened a very large loophole for a wide variety of (restrictive) preferential agreements (Jackson, 1989: 141).

It is, however, clear that RTAs are meant to be exceptions to the universal regime, not a rule nor was it meant to be practiced universally by all members. Yet, by June 2016 every WTO member had been a member of RTAs in force (WTO Regional, undated). As of 1 March 2022, there were 354 RTAs in force, with a total of 577 notifications from members to the WTO,[11] covering both trade in goods and services (WTO facts and Figures, undated). Further analysis indicates that the majority of these RTAs are bilateral, which are likely to have only limited impact on the global regulatory regime. These RTAs are more likely to meet the requirement that they remain complementary to, not a substitute for, the multilateral system.[12]

However, the recent emergence of the so-called super/mega RTAs (TPP/CPTPP, RCEP, TTIP and IPEF negotiations, etc.) – their emergence coinciding with the failure of negotiations for the development rounds and the

9 See, for instance, Lester, Mercurio, & Davies, 2018: 331; Matsushita, Schoenbaum, Mavroidis, & Hahn, 2015: 507. We have here followed the WTO practice of referring them to as regional trade agreements (RTAs). Further, preferential treatment agreement (PTA) is often used (including by the WTO) to refer to those unilateral trade preference agreements in which the developed nations grant, on a non-reciprocal basis, preferential treatment to developing countries. Thus, the use of PTA in this context could create some unnecessary confusion.

10 For a summary of the controversy and debate, see Lester, Mercurio, & Davies, 2018: 331–338; Matsushita, Schoenbaum, Mavroidis, & Hahn, 2015: 509–512.

11 See www.wto.org/english/tratop_e/region_e/region_e.htm#facts (last accessed 23/4/22).

12 On this requirement, see Para 28 of the Nairobi Ministerial Declaration, adopted on 19 December 2015, WT/MIN(15)/DEC, available at www.wto.org/english/thewto_e/minist_e/mc10_e/mindecision_e.htm (last accessed 8/11/21).

rise of emerging (especially Asian) economic powers[13] – and the increasing number of developing countries in RTAs suggest that some rather different explanations are needed to understand the phenomena that these RTAs which not only have overlapping memberships but also, at the same time, restrictive memberships. There is little doubt that they pose some serious challenge to the integrity and coherence of global regulation of trade and, with large number of countries/regions in their membership, they can hardly be said to be complementary to the traditional global trade (GATT and WTO) regulatory regime.

3. The Rising Powers and the New Challenge to International Economic Order

Chapter 2 concluded that, despite some limited successes in obtaining certain concessions in the form of S&D treatment, the first major challenges mounted by developing countries to the Western-dominated international economic order has largely been a failure. Clearly, these early challenges to the international economic order were mounted on the basis of the political capacities of the numerous developing countries, with willful disregard to the hugely different development status among them. Further, these developing countries had, at the time, little economic power to back up a sustained claim to alter the existing order. Finally, even though such challenges were made in the name of establishing an NIEO, they amounted to little more than obtaining some limited concessions or exceptions *within* the existing regime.

The rise of the Asian powers and other emerging economies presented a rather different scenario. Although the initial rise of the four 'Asian Tigers' (South Korea, Taiwan, Singapore and Hong Kong) did not lead to major demands for changes to the liberal international economic order, it nevertheless began a remarkable process of the shift of international economic power from West to Asia by the time of the establishment of the WTO. These changes have been described by some as 'tectonic shifts in the global balance of economic power' (Baracuhy, 2012: 108). In particular, the rise of India and China has led many to call the 21st century the 'Asian century' (Australian Government, 2012),[14] as opposed to the twentieth century, often considered as the American century (Enderwick, 2007: 172).[15] As the Indian

13 See the annual RTA notifications maintained by WTO regional trade database: www.wto.org/english/tratop_e/region_e/region_e.htm#facts (last accessed 9/11/21).

14 On the rise of China and India as new economic powerhouses, see Enderwick, 2007.

15 For more information on how the emerging economies in Asia have come to compete economically and politically with the United States, see generally de Silva, 2009: 34–72. See also Ramirez, 2006; Jacques, 2009; Hugh White, 2013.

and Chinese economies continue to rapidly climb the 'industrialisation ladder' (Gordon, 2009: 132; see also, Yusuf & Nabeshima, 2010), Asia has remained for some decades the most dynamic economic region in global economy, much more than just a 'self-contained strategic or economic system' (Australian Government, 2012: 46). The pace and scale of Asia's rise has been of such extent that it has literally changed the world (Australian Government, 2012: 40ff).[16] Perhaps, more accurately, the rise of Asia's economic power demands major changes in global governance. As a result, its 'growing weight is altering the focus of global governance' (Australian Government, 2012: 46) and is contributing to the creation of a new international economic order (Gordon, 2009: 131–162).

Obviously, there are many intrinsic and extrinsic factors that have contributed to the rise of Asia (see also Prestowitz, 2004). Suffice to say that the rise of Asia has led to the reduction of trade and investment barriers, thus transforming Asia into an economic hot spot. Further, the economic rise of Asia has caused changes affecting one of the traditional hegemons in global economic governance – the United States (Gordon, 2009: 132–133). This was especially so during the global financial crisis in 2008 and the subsequent demise of the global economic system, when Asia (especially China) was called upon to assist in rescuing the United States (Gordon, 2009: 160). In this context, Asian countries have, not surprisingly, demanded a larger role in global economic governance (Gordon, 2009: 132), logically driving the repositioning of powers in the multilateral trading system.

This shift in the global balance of economic power was further fuelled by the rapid development of emerging economies outside Asia, such as Brazil, Mexico and so on.[17] Together, the Asian powers and the emerging economies constitute the most important economic block, loosely referred to as the rising powers, in the post-war economic order. They began to change the rules of game in the political negotiations at the WTO and, in particular, the general dynamics of the (failed) Doha talks (Wouters & Burnay, 2012: 79. Karmakar, 2007: 61). With these new players in the game, the old powers of

16 According to the report, the rise of Asia has shifted global production, trade and investment; transformed commodity markets due to its rapid urbanisation; created a sophisticated innovation hub fostering technological development; and transformed consumer markets given its burgeoning middle class (see also Enderwick, 2007: 172–174). For more details on China's impact on the global economy, see Lardy, 2002; Economist, 2005; Defraigne, 2012: 13–49. For more information on the rise of India, see generally Cohen, 2001.

17 Neither the World Bank nor the IMF (nor the WTO) defines the notion of 'emerging economies/markets'. The notion is however widely used in financial and investment circles, referring to rapidly developing countries. For an early discussion of the notion by IMF, see Mody, 2004.

the 'Quad' (US, EU, Canada and Japan) could no longer shape the multilateral trading system exclusively as they did under the auspices of the GATT (Baracuhy, 2012: 108; Schott, 2010: 355). In a practical sense, it means that, if the United States and the European Union still remain influential in relation to the progress of the WTO negotiations (Niblett, 2012: 5), they no longer monopolise decision-making (Cohn, 2007: 212), especially when the old 'Quad' was replaced by the 'G-4' informal steering group of the Doha Round,[18] and the 'G-4' is not a homogenous 'club of like-minded countries' that the 'Quad' once was (Higgott, 2009: 11). It is rather 'a more diverse group of countries in the driving seat' (Narlikar, 2010: 722). This diversity has justified the fact that the emerging economies, such as Brazil, South Africa, India and China, now need to be on board during the negotiation and decision-making processes of any global trade regulatory regime.

The rising powers have actively sought to consolidate their place on the negotiating table by using technical device of the 'single undertaking' principle to their advantage. Ironically, this was the same principle that was used during the Uruguay Round by developed countries to force the hand of their developing counterparts. However, the single undertaking principle bit back, throughout the Doha talks, in that the same principle has given the emerging economies a *de facto* veto power at the WTO (Schott, 2009: 1; Narlikar, 2013a: 108). As a result of this 'over-democratisation' of the WTO system (Mattoo & Subramanian, 2011: 33), if the rising powers decide to oppose a particular outcome of the Doha Round, they can, in principle, block the progress of negotiations. In other words, the contribution by the rising powers can be a key element to the success of any international trade talks, just as it was a considerable force that led the Doha Round into an inevitable failure (Schott, 2009: 1). Equally, it is noteworthy that with new players there emerged new coalitions at the WTO aimed at curbing the hegemony of the United States and the European Union.[19] Among them, the emerging powers of China and India, both members of the 'G-20'[20] and 'BRICS',[21]

18 The phrase 'G-4' is used to refer to different groupings in different contexts, but it includes the United States, the European Union, India and Brazil in the present discussion (Schott, 2009: 6).

19 For a list of groups that are involved in WTO negotiations, see www.wto.org/english/tratop_e/dda_e/negotiating_groups_e.htm (7/6/22). For a general overview on the role of these coalitions during the WTO negotiations, see Tussie, 2009: 335–342. See also Hurell & Narlikar, 2006: 419–422; Narlikar, 2003.

20 A fairly united coalition of developing countries including China and India lobbying for a substantial reform on agriculture. It is different from the G20 of the Twenty Major Economies. For more information on the role of the 'G-20' coalition, see Narlikar & Tussie, 2004: 947–966.

21 BRICS includes the emerging economies of Brazil, Russia, India, China and South Africa.

played some critical roles in successfully achieving the blockage of Doha. Thus, in July 2008, China, which agreed to participate in the Doha steering group for the first time, teamed up with India to oppose farm reforms to their economies, thus diminishing any prospects for a breakthrough on the modalities for negotiating the liberalisation of agriculture (Schott, 2009: 8; Narlikar, 2011b: 1614).

This change of economic power has effectively taken the multilateral trading system to a critical juncture in terms of decision-making. Since the days of the GATT and until quite recently, the multilateral trade system was considered a 'bipolar system' (The Warwick Report, 2007: 13) dominated by the United States and the European Union, or a 'multilateral system' if the contribution of Japan is taken into account (Wouters & Burnay, 2012: 79). This system is now described as a 'multipolar alternative in which Brazil, China and India have asserted greater influence over the trajectory of the multilateral trading system' (The Warwick Report, 2007: 13), or even as Higgott maintains, 'a non-polar' system (Higgott, 2009: 8), in which the 'collective economic dominance [of the United States and the European Union] is giving way to a dispersal of economic power in a southerly and easterly direction' (Higgott, 2009: 10).

Regardless of how the system is described, 'multipolar' or 'non-polar', two major changes are clearly visible. First, the hierarchy of the international economic order has been widened to allow much bigger roles for participants, other than the usual major players, in setting up international trade policies (Gordon, 2009: 160). At the practical level, the cooperation between the United States and the European Union on the one side, and the BRICS on the other side is a mandatory precondition for the success of the Doha trade negotiations (see generally Schott, 2009: 1–22). Second, the leadership at the top of the hierarchy of the international economic order has been altered, as the dominance of the United States and the European Union has started to wane (Gordon, 2009: 161) and the roles of the emerging powers become much more visible.

4. The Doha Stalemate (and Failure) and the Shift to RTA

While it is said that the WTO has better coped with this shift in the balance of power than the two other Bretton Woods institutions of the IMF and the World Bank (Narlikar, 2011a: 112–114; Higgott, 2009: 11, *contra* Wouters & Burnay, 2012: 80), it has been clear that, from the Doha Round onwards, the WTO had been in a vicious circle of stalemate and inefficiency (Narlikar, 2010: 724–725, 2011a: 115). This stalemate ultimately ended unceremoniously with the failed Doha Round in 2015 and, as such, the international economic order is, in a significant sense, in limbo.

It is not uncommon, in Western media reporting, that the rising powers are often blamed for the failures at the Doha negotiations, believing that the inclusion of emerging economies such as India and China into the decision-making process has backfired (Narlikar, 2010: 720–725, 2011a: 115). The reality is much more complicated than it is perceived. In fact, the initial Doha agenda amounted to little more than the policy inertia of the Uruguay Round, completely ignoring the economic reality brought about by the rising powers. The inbuilt but defective decision-making mechanism at WTO ('consensus' and 'single undertaking') then provided a perfect means for the failure of its negotiations when the Western domination was replaced by the multi-polarisation of the world economy (Wouters & Burnay, 2012: 80).

In general, the attitude towards and perception of rising powers has been contradictory. On the one hand, emerging economies are seen as 'drivers of economic growth' and sought-after trade partners, but on the other hand, they are seen as 'nay-sayers' and 'disrupters' of the Doha Round and other trade negotiations (Narlikar, 2006: 60). This last perception is often attributed to the lack of compromise from India and China (Narlikar, 2010: 721, 2011a: 115; Schott, 2009: 10), especially on agriculture and their influences on other members of the BRICS into standing their ground against the demands of the traditionally leading decision-makers at the WTO. As such, it is claimed by some that the emergence of the 'rising powers' has driven the international economic order into a 'messy transition' phase (Higgott, 2009: 8). It is claimed that the international economic order has been transformed to a 'multipolar' one. The traits of this multipolar order are however, yet to be determined clearly as the international community waits for the dust of this new equilibrium of powers to settle down (see generally, Gordon, 2009: 131–162).

However, the Indian and Chinese experiences on the negotiating table are not quite the same as each other, in negotiating style, tactics and objectives. It is true that both countries implemented, for some decades, 'inward-looking' policies designed to promote 'self-sufficiency' with a socialist orientation, and both countries aspired and aspire to be a representative or leader of developing countries through their support for multilateralism. India has however been accused of showing 'a considerable willingness to 'Just Say No' with remarkable consistency' (Narlikar, 2006: 60), while China has been mostly described as a 'silent player' (Gao, 2012: 59) until quite recently when it started to favour activism after going through a strenuous 'listening and learning exercise' (Higgott, 2009: 12). China has also been accused of being a 'free-rider' through its 'low-profile' approach, yet

China's more assertive approach, from 2006 onwards, is also accused of being aggressive.[22]

The reality is that we are in a transitional period, with all powers trying to find a new equilibrium of power in establishing a new international economic order, and the existing and rising powers are still testing each other for co-existence. Searching for a new balance of powers is, however, only one of the factors contributing to the Doha failure. Fundamentally, the Doha 'development' agenda (or 'implementation' as understood in the WTO context) represents little more than old policies, originating from the initial challenge by developing countries to establish an NIEO. The Doha agenda failed to recognise the need for a new balance of power in regulating international trade and the hugely different trading capacities among 'developing countries'.

It is inevitable that a more differentiated approach, based on common interests and capacities, was to appear during the crisis of international trade talks, just like the period during which the Uruguay Round was in crisis. Critically different from RTAs resulting during the previous crises, a new species of RTA – the 'super agreements' – began to emerge that have the potential to change the nature of free trade agreements and, in most cases, also covering investment (liberalisation, protection, facilitation and cooperation and dispute resolution). These included at the time but were not limited to:

- the Trans-Pacific Partnership (TPP; now the CPTPP: a Comprehensive and Progressive Agreement for Trans-Pacific Partnership) (concluded);
- the Trans-Atlantic Trade and Investment Partnership (TTIP) (discontinued since April 2019);
- the Regional Comprehensive Economic Partnership (RCEP) (concluded); and
- the Trade in Services Agreement (TiSA) (no new negotiation since December 2016).

These agreements, many of which were then at a negotiation stage, are often described as 'mega-regional deals' that are historically unprecedented and would have a game-changing effect once taking effect. But, more fundamentally, such 'super regionalism' has always had a geopolitical element that is also intra-regional in nature.

22 For a detailed analysis of India's and China's negotiation behaviour and perceptions of their conduct, see Narlikar, 2011b, Gao, 2012.

5. The RTA Showdown and the Disintegration of International Economic Order?

The movement towards RTAs while the Doha Round was in stalemate is described as a 'silent migration' from the WTO system to alternative regional trade forums (Higgott, 2009: 21–25). Once again, this shift to regionalism is attributed, by some, to the rise of Asian powers and emerging economies. Specifically, in the view of some, given that the rise of BRICS has coincided with a new impetus in the general proliferation of regionalism (Schott, 2009: 8), the major players of the Asian-Pacific region could no longer be seen as the staunch supporters of multilateralism (Dieter, 2009a: 2). The reality, however, is that because of the growing politico-economic rivalry between the major developed and the rising powers on the international scene (Dieter, 2009a: 14), both 'camps' have started to place more emphasis on regionalism (Dieter, 2009a: 14). Members of BRICS are, in some respects, merely keeping up with the general trend towards regionalism in recent years (Seshadri, 2009: 921; Dasgupta, 2012). In fact, if there is a migration to regionalism (Dieter, 2009b: 393–408; Whalley, 2008: 517–532), it is also due to the large gap between the official rhetoric highlighting the importance of multilateralism that has been adopted by the United States and the European Union in international forums on the one hand, and their domestic trade policy leaning towards regionalism as well as protectionism on the other hand (Dieter, 2009a: 1–2, 11). The positions of India and China on multilateralism and regionalism are equally ambiguous.

Historically, India has always been loyal to a traditional multilateral approach, but the progressive erosion of the multilateral trading system has slowly changed India's stance on this matter (Mattoo & Subramanian, 2003: 333. Also; Chaisse, Chakraborty, & Nag, 2011; Farasat, 2008; Mehta & Narayanan, 2006; Jha, 2011; Nataraj, 2007). More specifically, since the late 1990s, India started showing 'greater openness' (Seshadri, 2009: 903) towards initiating bilateral negotiations with several countries (Whalley, 2008: 517; Chanda & Sasidaran, 2008). As its economy experienced rapid growth, it has felt confident to explore a parallel regional track of trade liberalisation with select partners (Seshadri, 2009: 903). As such, it is said, that India's openness towards RTAs has gone through three progressive phases. During the first phase, and up until 1998, 'RTAs were confined mainly to being preferential trade arrangements with developing countries that had limited scope' (Seshadri, 2009: 905–906). The second phase started with the conclusion of the India-Sri Lanka Free Trade Agreement. It was characterised by the negotiation of more comprehensive agreements with developing countries (Seshadri, 2009: 906–913). It was only during the third phase, said to have begun around 2005, that India started negotiating RTAs with developed countries in Asia (such as Japan) as part of its 'Look East' (see further, Chanda & Sasidaran, 2008: 3–12) policy and with several European Members of the OECD (Seshadri, 2009: 904, 913–916).

India's 'Look East' policy in the context of RTA has another objective in mind, that is, the rivalry with China for regional leadership. India takes the view that a limited RTA would not force it to confer the same MFN benefits to rival economies – such as China – as it would normally have to do under a prospective comprehensive WTO Doha deal (Schott, 2009: 10). Generally speaking, India's fear of a rising China has been a major driver to its regional strategies, especially its 'Look East' policy. India has sought to counterbalance China's economic influence and avoid marginalisation in Asia by negotiating RTAs with its neighbouring countries (Chanda & Sasidaran, 2008).[23] In other words, India's approach to regionalism is coloured by its geopolitical race with China to secure its position as a potential leader in Asia.

In relation to China, it can be argued that China has generally followed a similar path to India's. Although China had pledged to respect multilateralism upon its accession to the WTO, it has negotiated several RTAs since then (Whalley, 2008: 517, but *contra* Zhao, Malouche, & Newfarmer, 2008: 31). When China began to rise to a prominent position in the regional economy at the beginning of the 21st century, officials in Beijing became interested in further developing the existing trade networks with their neighbours in Northeast and Southeast Asia by negotiating several RTAs. Even after joining the WTO in 2001, the strategy by Beijing consisted in establishing regional trade arrangements with other countries in parallel to China's participation in the Doha Round negotiations (Zhao, Malouche, & Newfarmer, 2008: 22). It is thought that the Chinese enthusiasm for RTAs came as a reaction to the Asian financial crisis of 1997–1998 (Schott, 2009: 9). The rationale behind China's enthusiasm for RTAs was to develop regional responses to regional problems, rather than an ideological shift from WTO principles (Schott, 2009: 9). However, China's rise also triggered the advance of Asian regionalism (Schott, 2009: 9). More specifically, other Asian countries were compelled to emulate the Chinese overture to ASEAN (Kwei, 2006: 135). Asia soon became 'the current flashpoint of competitive regionalism' (Schott, 2009: 16). With this overwhelming trend of regionalism in Asia, scholars have highlighted the prospect of a large-scale regional trade agreement 'uniting the north-east and south-east Asia countries into

23 On rivalry between India and China and their potential cooperation in multilateral regimes, see Chen, 2010: 53–91

a large Asian trading bloc that could provide a "Plan B" if the WTO talks collapse' (Schott, 2009: 9).

In general, China's initial motivation to actively push its own free trade agreement (FTA) strategy was to counter-balance the growing influence of its rivals in East-Asia (Song & Yuan, 2012: 111–112). Its regional strategies were shaped around two focal points.[24] First, China's growing economic power has allowed it to employ a variety of tactics to achieve its interests in terms of regional security in Asia. To that end, as China's policy of opening to the outside world has entered a new stage (Cai, 2011: 155), it has sought a deeper economic integration with its counterparts in East Asia to assert the concept of 'China as an opportunity' rather than 'China as a threat' (Cai, 2011: 156).[25] Therefore, it can be argued that China's primary interest, at least initially, in regional trade agreements was equally motivated by its desire to achieve political stability in Asia (Wang, 2005: 50; Kwei, 2006: 135–136), and its quest for a 'peaceful ascendancy' to a great power (Wang, 2005: 52–54; Song & Wen, 2012: 112).

Second, China's regional approach has always involved a geo-political element. Politically, it is thought that regional trade connections have played a major role in enhancing its reputation in Asia. From a foreign policy perspective, China has largely benefited from strengthening regional economic cooperation with its neighbours around the time of the Asian financial crisis in 1997–1998. Nonetheless, despite China's efforts to present itself to its neighbours as 'a reliable bilateral economic partner' (Song & Wen, 2012: 112), China has failed to impress due to its 'unwillingness to solve territorial disputes in a multilateral setting' (Song & Wen, 2012: 114). Therefore, China's regional trade strategies have, from time to time, failed for reasons that are not strictly trade related. Economically, China has utilised RTAs as a mechanism to build trading relations with resource-exporting countries in order to secure the access to an adequate supply of energy and raw materials (Zhao, Malouche, & Newfarmer, 2008: 22). Even more, China has sought to remove the discrimination to which it was subjected to at the time of its accession to the WTO through the medium of RTAs (Lawrence, 2006). But importantly, China has also used these agreements as part of its defensive strategy to mitigate the economic effects of regional arrangements that exclude it (Zhao, Malouche, & Newfarmer, 2008: 22). At this stage, China's objectives were to secure

24 For more information on the motivations behind China's approach to regionalism, see Jiang, 2010: 238–261; Howe, 2007: 96–97.

25 On the emergence of China as an FTA hub in East Asia, see generally Park & Cheong, 2008: 106ff.

its long-term interests, regional stability and regional leadership, each of which is inter-related.

Importantly, however, China's race to negotiate RTAs with its neighbouring countries in the region has been attributed to 'the unresolved rivalry between China and Japan for leadership in Asia' (Dieter, 2009a: 14; Kwei, 2006: 136), and more recently between China and India. In other words, Asian regionalism has always had a geo-political aspect. It is, however, the competition with the United States over the establishment of a major regional trade agreement in the Asia-Pacific region that made the geopolitical politics intra-regional in nature. This is because the Obama Administration was then actively negotiating the TTP with major Asian countries, which excluded China (more generally, Hutchinson, 2012).[26]

When the 'super' RTAs, in the form of TPP, TTIP (both US led and promoted) and the RCEP (China's pan-regional agreement) began to emerge, the race to regionalism was then shaping up as a showdown between the existing and emerging powers (For geopolitical analyses and perceived significance of these RTAs, see Seshadri, 2013; Commonwealth, 2013; Jin, 2013; TPP India, 2013; Roy, 2013). The competition for regionalism now effectively changed the nature of the race to regionalism, as the rivalry is now of a global nature. While economic powers and interests still worked in the background, backing up claims for regional leadership, the global geopolitical rivalry was the force that pushed the existing powers and rising powers to a showdown in their efforts to establish a new international economic order, potentially causing the disintegration of the existing multilateral order under the auspices of the Bretton Woods system.

6. From Asia-Pacific to Indo-Pacific – The Naked Geopolitical Rivalry

While the Asian region has never seen any highly effective regional arrangement such as the EU, there is no shortage of regional mechanisms for political, economic and trade cooperation, with the RCEP being the most recent comprehensive arrangement. Further, with the participation of US, Canada, Russia, Mexico, Peru, Chile and so on, the region is often referred to as Asia-Pacific in general. Although rivalries and geopolitical competition has always been a factor in regional arrangements, the greater efforts were on cooperation, as demonstrated by the APEC (and the Free Trade Area of the Asia Pacific (FTAAP) therein) and the East Asia Summit (EAS). There

26 The geopolitical rivalry between the US and China and other China-related issues are to be discussed in the next chapter.

were once even talks about an Asia Pacific Community or an East Asian Community.[27] Even though the emergence of the super RTAs, but especially RCEP and TPP/CPTPP, signalled strong geopolitical rivalries, the battlefield was still on the ground of trade.

The rise of China, the existence of the deeply rooted rivalries among major powers (Japan, China and India) in Asia, and the geopolitical competition among world powers (China, US, Japan and India) eventually led to an entirely different set of considerations for Asia Pacific nations in terms of Asian regionalism (Chen, 2014: 377–402; Breslin, 2018). Thus came the most recent initiative,[28] the creation or, more precisely, the work-in-progress[29] project of creating an Indo-Pacific region (see Beeson & Lee-Brown, 2017), 'out of nothing, or very little, at least' (Beeson & Lee-Brown, 2017: 199; see also Tyler, 2014).

There are different conceptions as to what Indo-Pacific is and the notion remains controversial and contested (see Beeson & Lee-Brown, 2017: 200–201; Tyler, 2019; Ayres, 2018; Welti, Woker, & Bohn, 2018; Kuo, 2018; Tyler & Bachhawat, 2014; Dobell, 2019; Gyngell, 2018; Das, 2019; Manning, 2018). A prominent Australian scholar, head of the National Security College, ANU, Rory Medcalf argues that, as a region, Indo-Pacific is understood as 'an expansive definition of a maritime super-region centred on Southeast Asia, arising principally from the emergence of China and India as outward-looking trading states and strategic actors' (Medcalf, 2014: 474). He further elaborates:

> The idea of an Indo-Pacific region involves recognizing that the growing economic, geopolitical, and security connections between the Western Pacific and the Indian Ocean regions are creating a single "strategic system." At its simplest, this can be understood as a set of geopolitical power relationships among nations where major changes in one part of the system affects what happens in the others. In this sense, the Indo-Pacific can be understood as a maritime "super-region" with its geographical center in Southeast Asia.
>
> (footnotes omitted) (Medcalf, 2015)

27 For a detailed study of the debates on an Asia-Pacific regional architecture, see Murray, 2010.

28 Thus, it is asserted that the key factor in this development is the rise of China. See Beeson & Lee-Brown, 2017: 198. At least, as far as the American advocates of the Indo-Pacific idea are concerned, it is primarily conceived of as a response to the rise of China and the maintenance of American primacy. See Beeson & Wilson, 2018.

29 Others take the view that the Indo-Pacific is merely taking baby steps whereas the Asia-Pacific idea offers a reliable path dependence. See Chong & Wu, 2018.

For many who advocate the idea of an Indo-Pacific region, this is the way to keep the US strategically engaged in Asia while actively responding to the growing power and influence of China (Beeson & Lee-Brown, 2017: 196). Or as put bluntly by Beeson and Lee-Brown, 'the overwhelming rationale of the Indo-Pacific thus far has been strategic and geopolitical and designed to extend and reinforce American-led military primacy and to balance against the rise of China' (Beeson & Lee-Brown, 2017: 201). This geopolitical consideration means that the notion focuses on security which prevails over economic cooperation, the latter the foundation of the notion of Asia Pacific of the 1990s and 2000s (see Wilson, 2018: 3). As such, it is not surprising that 'Indo-Pacific' as a notion appears mostly in defence papers,[30] and it is principally promoted by the Quad – Australia, India, Japan and the US – with a prominent security/geopolitical emphasis.[31] However, to avoid conflict with the existing system of multilateral arrangements in Asia that centred around the ASEAN and established on economic foundations (Wilson, 2018: 5–8), the Indo-Pacific strategy needs to address economic concerns, in addition to security issues (Wilson, 2017).

After years of uncertainty, especially after the withdrawal from the TPP by the Trump Administration in 2017, the Biden Administration finally issued its Indo-Pacific Strategy in February 2022.[32] This Strategy explicitly singles out challenges from China as one of the reasons for the strategy, and outlines five objectives that include both economic prosperity and regional security, with much of the realisation of objectives yet to be worked out.

30 See Australia Defence White Paper 2013 (www.defence.gov.au/whitepaper/2013/docs/WP_2013_web.pdf (last accessed 20/7/19)), Australia Defence White Paper 2016 (www.defence.gov.au/WhitePaper/Docs/2016-Defence-White-Paper.pdf (last accessed 20/7/19)); Indo-Pacific Strategy Report: Preparedness, Partnerships, and Promoting a Networked Region, the Department of Defense, US, 1 June 2019 (https://media.defense.gov/2019/Jul/01/2002152311/-1/-1/1/DEPARTMENT-OF-DEFENSE-INDO-PACIFIC-STRATEGY-REPORT-2019.PDF (last accessed 20/7/19)), and *France and Security in the Indo-Pacific*, 2018 Edition, and updated in May 2019 (www.defense.gouv.fr/content/download/532754/9176250/file/France%20and%20Security%20in%20the%20Indo-Pacific%20-%202019.pdf (last accessed 20/7/19)).

31 It is said that, since 2010, these four countries have formally adopted the term Indo-Pacific into their foreign or defence policy. See Wilson, 2017: 2. Another strong advocate is Indonesia. See Marsudi (Foreign Minister of Indonesia), 2019. It should however also be pointed out that this term is increasingly being used by other countries, with the French government issuing an Indo-Pacific security paper in 2019 and the ASEAN began to embrace the term in June 2019 when it issued the 'ASEAN OUTLOOK ON THE INDO-PACIFIC' (a copy of the document is available at www.asean2019.go.th/en/news/asean-outlook-on-the-indo-pacific/). See also Tyler, 2019; Ayres, 2018.

32 A copy is available at www.whitehouse.gov/wp-content/uploads/2022/02/US-Indo-Pacific-Strategy.pdf (last accessed 16/6/22).

Three months later, the US finally launched the Indo-Pacific Economic Framework for Prosperity (IPEF) on 23 May 2022 (Joint Statement, 2022). Symbolically, it was launched in Japan just before the 2022 Quad meeting. Its initial partners include Australia, Brunei, India, Indonesia, Japan, Republic of Korea, Malaysia, New Zealand, the Philippines, Singapore, Thailand and Vietnam, said to represent 40% of the world's GDP.[33]

The IPEF is, however, not a traditional market access and trade liberalisation treaty. It is a framework to negotiate agreements on identified issues. At the moment, the identified areas for cooperation include, but are not limited to, digital economy, labour standards, environmental protection, clean energy and decarbonisation, global supply chains, and corporate tax and anti-corruption regimes. These subject-matters are clearly not about trade liberalisation, but critical issues where standards for international trade are yet to be established. Not surprising, the language is 'to decide on rules of the road' among like-minded allies (Fact Sheet, 2022) – this was the typical language used during the TPP negotiation.

However, the most important aspect of IPEF is the one that is not spoken about, that is, the exclusion of China. Effectively, it is the Biden Administration's replacement for the TPP, with an entirely different approach to trade issues that emphasises shared values among 'allies' (Fact Sheet, 2022; Strangio, 2022). This time around, there has been very little effort among the main initiators, namely the Quad led by the US, to hide their geopolitical objectives in establishing such a framework. China, of course, understands these Quad geopolitical objectives, wasting no time to attack the Framework as a coercive tool to compel others to serve the purposes of the US geopolitical strategy (MFA, 2022). The Chinese Minister of Foreign Affairs now questions whether the US is politicising, weaponising and ideologising economic issues and coercing regional countries to take sides by economic means (Wang Yi, 2022; Overly, 2022). In short, the RTA showdown between political powers is now open geopolitical warfare, a subject matter of next chapter.

7. Conclusion

On the surface, the RTA movement is a continuing process in the struggle for an NIEO by developing countries. In truth, the RTA movement is caused by the changing of the balance of economic powers, not just political ones, as in the NIEO movement.

33 The IPEF is open for participation and, indeed, Fiji soon joined after the initial launch in May 2022.

There are many factors that make the present challenge to international economic order different from the NIEO efforts, but two are particularly relevant in this context. First, the size of Asian countries and their economies and their rapid economic development in the last three decades or so have seen a massive shift of wealth from the West to Asia, making Asia the undisputable engine of world economic development. As a result, India and China will eventually become economic superpowers of the world in the foreseeable future. Secondly, the world economy is also in transformation and transition from manufacturing to services, led by the technological revolution and innovation, with technological innovation spreading rapidly on a global scale in this age of information revolution. While the US and, to a lesser extent, the EU led the technological revolution and still has some advantages over Asia, the gap is being filled rapidly, as utilisation and commercialisation of technologies are as important and valuable as technological innovation itself.

The shift from manufacturing to services necessarily demands major changes to be made to the existing international trading rules (which for a long time focused on trade in goods), and the rising powers logically want a role in the design of such rules and mechanisms. Together with their demands to have more decision-making powers in other international economic institutions, such as the IMF and the World Bank, the challenge to the existing international economic order is no longer an academic topic; it is a political reality that needs to be addressed carefully. This challenge, in strong contrast to the previous challenges from developing countries, is now backed up by economic power.

Much has been said about the stalemate/failure at the Doha negotiations. It is, however, worthwhile pointing out that, as opined by Baracuhy, the Doha deadlock is nothing but 'a microcosm of the rising tensions between old and new powers and the challenges of continuity and change in the international order' (Baracuhy, 2012: 108). As such, as maintained by Baracuhy, the real issue to debate should revolve around an 'emerging global governance gap in the international system' (Baracuhy, 2012: 108). Accommodating rising powers does not have to result in the creation of a new divide between geopolitical powers. Given the level of economic interdependence between states, the main challenge to international economic governance is to build common rules and adapt the existing international institutions to mitigate the effects of the most recent changes to the international legal order (Niblett, 2012). In other words, making changes to international economic governance needs not undermine the necessity of cooperation between the old and rising powers at the WTO (Higgott, 2009: 8–9; Wang, 2012: 101).

Much has also been written in terms of the need to share power among the emerging and the existing powers to avoid conflict or even war in a race to hegemon (Enderwick, 2007; de Silva, 2009; Ramirez, 2006; Jacques, 2009; White, 2013). Clearly, the search for a new balance of power in the international economic order has led to a twisted development – the resurrection of RTA (in fact, super RTA) with a geopolitical balance of power in mind. These latest developments in RTA are, in many respects, fundamentally different from the RTA movement during the time of Uruguay Round negotiations. Trade, or liberalisation of trade, is no longer the ultimate goal, and this is especially true in the case of IPEF. There is little doubt that the TPP/CPTPP, RCEP and the IPEF have a potential to fundamentally undermine multilateralism in favour of opposing trade blocs more for geopolitical consideration than for trade liberalisation and, thus a potential to start a trade-led 'cold war'. If this happens, it will not be in the interest of any party involved.

References

Aggarwal, Vinod & Urata, Shujiro (eds.) (2006), *Bilateral Trade Agreements in the Asia-Pacific: Origins, Evolution, and Implications* (New York/London: Routledge).

Australian Government (2012), *Australia in the Asian Century 2012 – White Paper* (Canberra: Australian Government).

Ayres, Alyssa (2018), 'The quad and the free and open Indo-pacific', November 20, available at www.cfr.org/blog/quad-and-free-and-open-indo-pacific (last accessed 27/6/19).

Baracuhy, Braz (2012), 'Running into a brick wall: The WTO Doha round, governance gap and geopolitical risks', 3 (1) *Global Policy* 108.

Beeson, Mark & Lee-Brown, Troy (2017), 'The future of Asian regionalism: Not what it used to be?' 4 (2) *Asia & the Pacific Policy Studies* 195.

Beeson, Mark & Wilson, Jeffrey (2018), 'The Indo-pacific: Reconceptualising the Asian regional space', 35 (1) *East Asia*, available at www.researchgate.net/publication/324615046_The_Indo-Pacific_Reconceptualizing_the_Asian_Regional_Space (last accessed 19/7/19).

Breslin, Shaun (2018), 'Conceptualising Asian regionalism', (Dec) (RISE series #22), available at www.twai.it/wp-content/uploads/2018/11/Tnote73.pdf (last accessed 18/7/19).

Cai, Kevin (2011), 'China and economic regionalism in East Asia' in Shaw, Grant, & Cornelissen (2011).

Chaisse, Julien, Chakraborty, Debashis & Nag, Biswajit (2011), 'The three-pronged strategy of India's preferential trade policy', 26 (2) *Connecticut Journal of International Law* 415.

Chanda, Rupa & Sasidaran, G. (2008), 'Understanding India's regional initiatives within Asia', Working Paper No 48, Institute of South Asian Studies, National University of Singapore, 15 August.

Chen, Jianfu (2010), 'China, India and developing countries in the WTO: Towards a pro-active strategy', in Sornarajah & Wang (2010).

Chen, Jianfu (2014), 'Regional trade agreement in context', in Hu & Vanhullebusch (2014).

Chong, Alan & Wu, Shang-Su (2018), 'Two templates of Trans Asian regionalism', March, available at www.nst.com.my/opinion/columnists/2018/03/342278/two-templates-trans-asian-regionalism (last accessed 28/6/19).

Cohen, Stephen (2001), *India: Emerging Power* (New York: Brookings Institution Press).

Cohn, Theodore (2007), 'The world trade organization and global governance', in Lee & McBride (2007), 201.

Commonwealth (2013), 'Mapping the Terrain: Strengthening commonwealth economic cooperation: Potential implications of the Trans-Pacific Partnership (TPP) and the Regional Economic Cooperation Partnership (RCEP) free trade agreement on commonwealth small states and LDC', available at http://secretariat.thecommonwealth.org/job/191203/167709/257297/ead_pbcwg_0664.htm (last accessed 21/12/13).

Cottier, Thomas & Elsig, Manfred (eds.) (2011), *Governing the World Trade Organization: Past, Present and Beyond Doha* (New York: Cambridge University Press).

Das, Udayan (2019), 'What is the Indo-pacific?' 13 July, available at https://thediplomat.com/2019/07/what-is-the-indo-pacific/ (last accessed 19/7/19).

Dasgupta, Pinaki (2012), 'India and East Asia: Towards a regional economic integration', Paper presented at the Symposium on the 'Japan-India Relations in the 21st Century Asia Pacific Era', Japan Institute for Social and Economic Affairs, Tokyo, 16–19 January, available at www.kkc.or.jp/english/activities/indianscholars/KKC_FINAL_PAPER_PDG_.pdf (last accessed 8/02/14).

de Silva, Dharma (2009), 'Building BRICKS of the new global economy, competition and trading system', 14 (4) *Sri Lankan Journal of Management* 34.

Defraigne, Jean-Christophe (2012), 'China shakes the world: Challenges arising from shifts in the global balance of power', in Wouters et al. (2012), 13–49.

Dieter, Heribert (2009a), 'The decline of global economic governance and the role of the transatlantic powers', 11 (3) *Business and Politics* 1.

Dieter, Heribert (2009b), 'The multilateral trading system and preferential trade agreements: Can the negative effects be minimized?'15 (1) *Global Governance* 393.

Dobell, Graeme (2019), 'Indo-Pacific: From construct to contest', 24 June, available at www.aspistrategist.org.au/indo-pacific-from-construct-to-contest/ (last accessed 19/7/19).

Economist (2005), 'China and the world economy: From T-shirts to T-bonds', *Economist*, available at www.economist.com/node/4221685 (last accessed 17/10/13).

Enderwick, Peter (2007), *Understanding Emerging Markets: China and India* (New York/London: Routledge).

Fact Sheet (2022), 'FACT SHEET: In Asia, President Biden and a Dozen Indo-pacific partners launch the indo-pacific economic framework for prosperity', *The White House*, 23 May 2022, available at www.whitehouse.gov/briefing-room/

statements-releases/2022/05/23/fact-sheet-in-asia-president-biden-and-a-dozen-indo-pacific-partners-launch-the-indo-pacific-economic-framework-for-prosperity/ (last accessed 24/5/22).

Farasat, Shadan (2008), 'India's quest for regional trade agreements: Challenges ahead', 42 (3) *Journal of World Trade* 433.

Gao, Henry (2012), 'From the periphery to the Centre: China's participation in WTO negotiations', 1 *China Perspectives* 59.

Gordon, Ruth (2009), 'The dawn of a new, new international economic order?' 72 (4) *Law and Contemporary Problems* 131.

Gyngell, Allan (2018), 'To each their own Indo-pacific', 29 May, available at www.internationalaffairs.org.au/australianoutlook/to-each-their-own-indo-pacific/ (last accessed 19/7/19).

Hart, Andrew & Jones, Bruce (2010), 'How do rising powers rise?' 52 (6) *Survival: Global Politics and Strategy* 63.

Higgott, Richard (2009), 'Not just a "second order" problem in a wider economic crisis: Systemic challenges for the global trading system', 11 (3) *Business and Politics* 1.

Howe, Christopher (2007), 'Free trade areas and economic integration in East Asia: The view from China', in Siddique (2007).

Hu, Jiaxiang & Vanhullebusch, Matthias (eds.) (2014), *Regional Cooperation and Free Trade Agreements in Asia* (London/Leiden: Brill Nijhoff).

Hurell, Andrew & Narlikar, Amrita (2006), 'A new politics of confrontation? Brazil and India in multilateral trade negotiations', 20 (4) *Global Society* 415.

Hutchinson, Benjamin (2012), *China and the Trans-Pacific Partnership: Excluding One of the United States' Top Trading Partners from a Cross-Pacific Trade Preference Program?* (January: SelectedWorks), available at http://works.bepress.com/cgi/viewcontent.cgi?article=1003&context=benjamin_hutchinson (last accessed 17/10/13).

Jackson, John H. (1989), *The World Trading System: Law and Policy of International Economic Relations* (Cambridge, MA: The MIT Press).

Jacques, Martin (2009), *When China Rules the World: The End of the Western World and the Birth of a New Global Order*, 2nd edition (New York: Penguin Books).

Jha, Sejuti (2011), 'Utility of regional trade agreements: Experience from India's Regionalism', Working Paper No 99, Asia-Pacific Research and Training Network on Trade, April 2011, available at www.unescap.org/tid/artnet/pub/wp9911.pdf (last accessed 17/10/13).

Jiang, Yang (2010), 'China's pursuit of free trade agreements: Is China exceptional?' 17 (2) *Review of International Political Economy* 238.

Jin, Jianmin (2013), 'RCEP vs. TPP', available at http://jp.fujitsu.com/group/fri/en/column/message/2013/2013-02-22.html (last accessed 21/12/13).

Joint Statement (2022), 'Joint statement on Indo-pacific economic framework for prosperity', 23 May 2022, available at www.dfat.gov.au/news/media-release/launch-indo-pacific-economic-framework-prosperity-ipef-joint-statement (last accessed 24/5/22).

Karmakar, Suparna (2007), 'From Uruguay round to Doha: India at the negotiating table', in Karmakar, Kumar & Debroy (eds.), (2007).

Karmakar, Suparna, Kumar, Rajiv & Debroy, Bibek (eds.) (2007), *India's Liberalisation Experience: Hostage to the WTO?* (New Delhi: Sage Publications).

Keck, A. & Low, P. (2004), 'Special and differential treatment in the WTO: Why, when and how', WTO Staff Working Paper ERSD-2004–03. A PDF text is available from the WTO website: www.wto.org/english/res_e/reser_e/ersd200403_e.htm (last accessed 1/08/05).

Kuo, Mercy A. (2018), 'The origin of "Indo-pacific" as geopolitical construct', January, available at https://thediplomat.com/2018/01/the-origin-of-indo-pacific-as-geopolitical-construct/ (last accessed 27/6/19).

Kwei, Elaine (2006), 'Chinese trade bilateralism: Politics still in command', in Aggarwal & Urata (2006).

Langhelle, Oluf (ed.) (2013), *International Trade Negotiations and Domestic Politics: The Intermestic Politics of Trade Liberalization* (New York: Routledge).

Lardy, Nicholas (2002), *Integrating China into the Global Economy* (New York: Brookings Institution Press).

Lawrence, Robert (2006), 'China and the multilateral trading system', Working Paper No 12759, National Bureau of Economic Research, December.

Lee, Simon & McBride, Stephen (eds.) (2007), *Neo-Liberalism, State Power and Global Governance* (Germany: Springer).

Leong, Ho Khai & Ku, Samuel C. Y. (eds.) (2005), *China and Southeast Asia: Global Changes and Regional Challenges* (Singapore: Institute of Southeast Asian Studies).

Lester, Simon, Mercurio, Bryan & Davies, Arwel (2018), *World Trade Law: Text, Materials and Commentary*, 3rd edition (Oxford: Hart Publishing)

Manning, Robert A. (2018), 'US Indo-pacific strategy be careful what you wish for', December 2018, available https://eng.globalaffairs.ru/number/US-Indo-Pacific-Strategy-19916 (last accessed 20/7/19).

Marsudi, Retno L. P. (Foreign Minister of Indonesia) (2019), 'Insight: Time to deepen Indo-Pacific cooperation', *Jakarta*, 20 March, available at www.thejakartapost.com/academia/2019/03/20/insight-time-to-deepen-indo-pacific-cooperation.html (last accessed 27/6/19).

Matsushita, M., Schoenbaum, T. J., Mavroidis, P. C. & Hahn, M. (2015), *The World Trade Organization: Law, Practice, and Policy*, 3rd edition (Oxford: Oxford University Press)

Mattoo, Aaditya & Stern, Robert (eds.) (2003), *India and the WTO* (Washington: World Bank).

Mattoo, Aaditya & Subramanian, Arvind (2003), 'India and the multilateral trading system post-Doha: Defensive or proactive?' in Mattoo and Stern (2003).

Mattoo, Aaditya & Subramanian, Arvind (2011), 'China and the world trading system', Working Paper No 5897, World Bank, December.

Medcalf, Rory (2014), 'In defence of the Indo-pacific: Australia's new strategic map', 68 (4) *Australian Journal of International Affairs* 470.

Medcalf, Rory (2015), 'Reimagining Asia: From Asia-pacific to Indo-pacific', *Open Forum*, 26 June, available at www.theasanforum.org/reimagining-asia-from-asia-pacific-to-indo-pacific/ (last accessed 27/6/19).

Mehta, Rajesh & Narayanan, S. (2006), 'India's regional trading arrangements', Discussion Paper No 114, Research and Information System for Developing Countries, August.

MFA (2022), 'Press conference', 25 May 2022, Ministry of Foreign Affairs, available at www.mfa.gov.cn/web/fyrbt_673021/202205/t20220525_10692555.shtml (last accessed 28/5/22).

Mody, Ashoka (2004), 'What is an emerging market?' IMF WP/04/177, September, available at www.imf.org/external/pubs/ft/wp/2004/wp04177.pdf (last accessed 28/4/22).

Murray, Philomena (2010), *Regionalism and Community: Australia's Options in the Asian-Pacific* (Canberra: The Australian Strategic Policy Institute).

Narlikar, Amrita (2003), *International Trade and Developing Countries: Bargaining Coalitions in the GATT and WTO* (London/New York: Routledge).

Narlikar, Amrita (2006), 'Peculiar chauvinism or strategic calculation? Explaining the negotiating strategy of a rising India', 82 (1) *International Affairs* 59.

Narlikar, Amrita (2010), 'New powers in the club: The challenges of global trade governance', 86 (3) *International Affairs* 717.

Narlikar, Amrita (2011a), 'Adapting to new power balances: Institutional reform in the WTO', in Cottier & Elsig (2011).

Narlikar, Amrita (2011b), 'Is India a responsible great power?' 32 (9) *Third World Quarterly* 1607.

Narlikar, Amrita (2013a), 'India's trade politics: Continuity and change', in Langhelle (2013).

Narlikar, Amrita (2013b), 'Introduction: Negotiating the rise of new powers', 89 (3) *International Affairs* 561.

Narlikar, Amrita & Tussie, Dianna (2004), 'The G20 at the Cancun ministerial meeting: Developing countries and their evolving coalitions', 27 (7) *World Economy* 947.

Nataraj, Geethanjali (2007), 'Regional trade agreements in the Doha round: Good for India?' Discussion Paper No 67, Asian Development Bank Institute, May 2007, available at www.adbi.org/files/dp67.regional.trade.agreements.doha.pdf (last accessed 17/10/13).

Niblett, Robin (2012), 'The economic crisis and the emerging powers: Towards a new international order?' Working Paper, 20 February 2012, available at https://www.files.ethz.ch/isn/142782/0212niblett.pdf (last accessed 20/5/22).

Overly, Steven (2022), 'Your move, Beijing: US-China trade rivalry intensifies after Biden launches Asian economic pact', 26 May, available at www.politico.com/news/2022/05/26/us-china-trade-rivalry-biden-asian-economic-pact-00035232 (last accessed 27/5/22).

Park, Yung Chul & Cheong, Inkyo (2008), 'The proliferation of FTAs and prospects for trade liberalization in East Asia', in Eichengreen, Park & Wyplosz (2008).

Prestowitz, Clyde (2004), 'The great reverse – Part I', *YaleGlobal*, 2 September, available at http://yaleglobal.yale.edu/content/great-reverse-part-i (last accessed 17/10/13).

Ramirez, Steven (2006), 'Endogenous growth theory, status quo efficiency, and globalization', 17 (1) *Berkeley La Raza Law Journal* 1.

Roy, Anjian (2013), 'Bali is over, now look to the TPP summit in Singapore and beyond', 17 December, available at www.dnaindia.com/analysis/column-bali-is-over-now-look-to-the-tpp-summit-in-singapore-and-beyond-1936412 (last accessed 21/12/13).

Schott, Jeffrey (2009), 'America, Europe, and the new trade order', 11 (3) *Business and Politics* 1.

Schott, Jeffrey (2010), 'Does the WTO need to change?' 109 (730) *Current History* 355.

Seshadri, V. S. (2009), 'Evolution in India's regional trading arrangements', 43 (5) *Journal of World Trade* 903.

Seshadri, V. S. (2013), 'Three deals that can change the world', available at www.thehindu.com/opinion/lead/three-deals-that-can-change-the-world/article5207438.ece (last accessed 21/12/13).

Shaw, Timothy, Grant, Andrew & Cornelissen, Scarlett (eds.) (2011), *The Ashgate Research Companion to Regionalisms* (UK/US: Ashgate).

Siddique, M. A. B. (ed.) (2007), *Regionalism, Trade and Economic Development in the Asia-Pacific Region* (Cheltenham, UK & Northampton, MA, US: Edward Elgar).

Song, Guoyou & Yuan, Wen Jin (2012), 'China's free trade agreement strategies', 35 (4) *Washington Quarterly* 107.

Sornarajah, M. & Wang, Jiangyu (eds.) (2010), *China, India and the International Economic Order* (New York: Cambridge University Press).

Strangio, Sebastian (2022), 'Southeast Asian nations roll the dice on Biden's Indo-pacific framework', *The Diplomat*, May 24, available at https://thediplomat.com/2022/05/southeast-asian-nations-roll-the-dice-on-bidens-indo-pacific-framework/ (last accessed 25/5/22).

TPP India (2013); 'Trans-pacific partnership: An Indian perspective', available at www.maritimeindia.org/srtc_report.html (last accessed 21/12/13).

Trebilcock, M. J. & Howse, R. (1999), *The Regulation of International Trade*, 2nd edition (London/New York: Routledge).

Tussie, Diana (2009), 'Process drivers in trade negotiations: The role of research in the path to grounding and contextualizing', 15 (3) *Global Governance* 335.

Tyler, Melissa Conley (2014), 'Different visions of the Indo-Pacific: China, India, the US and Australia', available at www.lowyinterpreter.org/the-interpreter/different-visions-indo-pacific-china-india-us-and-australia (last accessed 30/6/19).

Tyler, Melissa Conley (2019), 'The Indo-Pacific is the New Asia', available at www.lowyinstitute.org/the-interpreter/indo-pacific-new-asia (last accessed 29/6/19).

Tyler, Melissa Conley & Bachhawat, Aakriti (2014), 'In a cleft stick: Australia's Indo-Pacific policy', January, available at www.aspistrategist.org.au/in-a-cleft-stick-australias-indo-pacific-policy/ (last accessed 30/6/19).

Wang, Jiangyu (2005), 'The legal and policy considerations of China-ASEAN FTA: The impact on the multilateral trading system', in Leong & Ku (2005).

Wang, Xiaodong (2012), 'What lessons can be learned from the Doha round', in Wouters et al. (2012).

Wang, Yi (2022), 'Wang Yi: We need to impose a big question mark over US 'Indo-Pacific Economic Framework', 22 May, available at www.mfa.gov.cn/wjbzhd/202205/t20220522_10690866.shtml (last accessed 28/6/22).

The Warwick Report (2007), *The Multilateral Trade Regime: Which Way Forward-Report of the First Warwick Commission* (UK: University of Warwick).

Welti, Philippe, Woker, Daniel & Bohn, Jeffrey (2018), 'Far from geography: A "free and open Indo-Pacific" ', September, available at https://asiasociety.org/switzerland/far-geography-free-and-open-indo-pacific (last accessed 27/6/19).

Whalley, John (2008), 'Recent regional agreements: Why so many, why so much variance in form, why coming so fast, and where are they headed', 31 (4) *World Economy* 517.

White, Hugh (2013), *The China Choice: Why America Should Share Power*, 2nd edition (Melbourne: Black Inc.).

Wilson, Jeffrey D. (2017), 'Investing in the economic architecture of the Indo-Pacific', (August) 8 *Indo-Pacific Insight Series*.

Wilson, Jeffrey D. (2018), 'A new region? Building partnerships for cooperative institutions in the Indo-Pacific: Report form the Perth US-Asia Centre Australia-US Indo-Pacific strategy conference', 13 April, available at https://perthusasia.edu.au/getattachment/9c43cb4d-7943-4110-9225-c4322753f02a/PU-57-Outcome-Report-WEB.pdf.aspx?lang=en-AU (last accessed 20/7/19).

Wouters, Jan & Burnay, Matthieu (2012), 'China and the European union in the world trade organization: Living apart together?' in Wouters et al. (2012).

Wouters, Jan et al. (eds.) (2012), *China, the European Union and Global Governance* (New York: Edward Elgar Publishing).

WTO (2014), 'Help WTO keep up the Bali momentum, Azevêdo asks parliamentarians', 12 February, available at www.wto.org/english/news_e/spra_e/spra7_e.htm (last accessed 20/02/14).

WTO Facts and Figures (undated), 'Facts and figures', available at www.wto.org/english/tratop_e/region_e/region_e.htm (last accessed 5/11/21).

WTO Regionalism (undated), 'Regionalism: Friends or rivals?' available at www.wto.org/english/thewto_e/whatis_e/tif_e/bey1_e.htm (last accessed 5/11/21).

Yusuf, Shahid & Nabeshima, Kaoru (2010), *Changing the Industrial Geography in Asia: The Impact of China and India* (Washington: World Bank Publications).

Zhao, Longyue, Malouche, Mariem & Newfarmer, Richard (2008), 'China's emerging regional trade policy', 1 (1) *Journal of Chinese Economic Foreign Trade Studies* 21.

4 Geopolitical and Geo-Economic Manoeuvring

The Rise of China

1. Introduction

As discussed in Chapter 3, China's participation in regional trade agreements (RTAs) has always had a geopolitical dimension. In fact, as a powerful trading nation with a politico-economic system that rejects many of the assumptions for a liberal economic order, China's rise, but especially its demand for leadership roles in international governance is, by definition, going to be controversial. On the one hand, it is not unreasonable that China, as a rising power with great trading capacities, demands a fair share of decision-making power in the shaping of international economic order. On the other hand, it is not surprising that existing powers are becoming increasingly anxious about and concerned with China's increasingly assertive stand on matters important to international trade and investment as they often see such a stand on geo-economic behaviour as being in support of China's geopolitical contest and manoeuvring.

While the rise of China raises many complicated and complex questions, two prominent strategies are likely to have major impact on the liberal international economic order. These are China's 'One Belt One Road' Initiative (hereinafter the BRI) and its increasing use of economic powers against countries that do not always agree with China's geopolitical aims. While it is difficult to predict the future of the more recent 'decoupling' (from China) strategies, the need for diversification is now widely felt globally, reflecting the on-going geopolitical struggles as well as market forces. There is little doubt that the rise of China poses some serious, if not the most serious, challenges to the liberal foundation of the multilateral trade regime.

This chapter first analyses the Chinese Belt and Road Initiative (BRI) as investment projects and as a geopolitical strategy. It then examines China's geo-economic manoeuvre in BRI and in international relations more generally, as well as the so-called 'decoupling' 'strategy' in the geopolitical and

DOI: 10.4324/9781003275510-5

geo-economic struggle.[1] This chapter concludes that China's rise has so far proven to mount the most serious challenge to the liberal international economic order, and there is yet no sign of the end of the geopolitical struggle between China and the existing powers led by the US.

2. Geopolitical Strategy: The Belt and Road Initiative (BRI)

2.1. BRI as Controversial Infrastructural Investment Projects

Ever since it was first announced by China in 2013 and officially implemented in 2015, the BRI has had some mixed results.[2] This should be neither surprising nor alarming considering the scale of the investment being implemented or planned and the large number of countries and international organisations involved. Indeed, the BRI is often referred to as a Trillion-Dollar Initiative. In today's value, the BRI investment is said to be seven times the size of the United States Marshall Plan to rebuild Europe after World War II (Smith, 2018),[3] or 12 times that of the Marshall Plan according to another calculation (Bowen, 2016: 7).[4] As of March 2022, China had signed just over 200 cooperation agreements with 149 countries and 32 international organisations to participate, to various extents and in different forms and nature,[5] in the implementation of the Initiative (BRI Country List, 2022). When one considers that China only started meaningful outward investment in the 1990s (Chen, 2016a: Ch 19), it should be expected that there would be a steep learning curve for all participants in the BRI and that many aspects of its practice appear to be controversial.[6]

1 China's recent use of economic powers against selected countries is discussed in Chapter 5 on dispute resolution.

2 Understandably, the Chinese Government and its official media has portrayed great achievements of the BRI so far. See BRI Five Years, 2019. Since the five-year report, Chinese media has periodically reported BRI achievements and many of these reports can be found in the dedicated BRI website: www.yidaiyilu.gov.cn. Western media, however, have given some rather different descriptions. For some recent and comprehensive reports, see Russel & Berger, 2020; Dossani, Bouey, & Zhu, 2020. It should also be pointed out that the BRI is undoubtedly a long-term strategy of the Communist Party of China (CPC), which was written into the CPC Constitution in October 2017. The commitment of the CPC and the Chinese government to the Initiative is therefore serious. See Tao & Zhong, 2018: 306–308

3 It should be pointed out, however, that 90 percent of the Marshall Plan was aid, whereas the BRI is mainly loans. See Bowen, 2016: 7.

4 Still another source puts it as 50 times of that of the Marshall Plan. See Manuel, 2019.

5 For an excellent analysis of these agreements, see Wang, 2021.

6 For an analysis of BRI's controversial practice, see Wang & Chen, 2020; Zhao, 2016; Li, 2019: 1–16.

Although China has claimed that some 149 countries have some kind of agreement to participate in the BRI implementation, it is opposed by some major economies in the world. India, for example, has shown little enthusiasm for the BRI, and Japan launched its own competing scheme not long after the BRI was launched.[7] Australia, being a middle power in the Asia-Pacific, has not only resisted Chinese suggestions to 'formally align' its AU$5 billion Australia Northern Infrastructure Strategy with the BRI (Daly, 2017; Golley & Ingle, 2018: 58), it actually, recently, cancelled an agreement signed between an Australian State government and the Chinese government (Varano, 2021).

Certain alternatives to the BRI have also been developed by other groups of nations. In July 2018, the US, Japan and Australia announced that they were forming a new trilateral partnership to build infrastructure in the Indo-Pacific. In announcing the new agreement, US Secretary of State Mike Pompeo stressed that the US was seeking 'partners, not domination'. At the same time, the then Australian Trade Minister Steve Ciobo emphasised that Australia's programs would only add to the existing regional programs. No one even mentioned China or the BRI, but everyone tacitly understood that this new partnership was a direct competitor against, if not a challenge to, the BRI,[8] and that this was just the beginning.[9] A year later (in November 2019), this trilateral partnership was formalised as the Blue Dot Network (McCawley, 2019), and in February 2020 India agreed to join the Network (Varano, 2021). In June 2021, the Group of Seven (G7) and the US announced a global infrastructure initiative, called Build Back Better, which clearly aims at giving the BRI 'a shot across the bow' (Arha, 2021. For details, see G7 Leaders' Communique, 2021).

In Europe, many European Union members have also rejected the BRI. In April 2018, it was reported that a joint report was signed by 27 (out of 28) EU member state ambassadors to China, criticising the BRI, though not rejecting the Initiative outright (EU Ambassadors, 2018; Corre, 2017; Viktor, 2017; Prasad, 2018).[10] Although not completely united as an entity

7 The Japanese scheme involved US$110 billion, exceeding the initial capitalisation of the Asian Infrastructure Investment Bank (AIIB). See Fujiwara, 2018.

8 The committed fund, so far, is only tiny compared to China's commitment to the Initiative. See McCulloch, 2018; Rogin, 2018.

9 Additionally, Australia has now allocated the largest slice of its foreign aid budget to the Pacific. See CNBC, 2018. Despite many headline-generating reports about China's investment in the Pacific, Australia and New Zealand combined contribute more than half of foreign aid in the Pacific, whereas until now China only has a share of eight per cent. See Wroe, 2018b.

10 Even Russia began to criticise the BRI. See Fang, 2018.

(Divided Europe, 2019; Kavalski & Mayer, 2019), the EU as a bloc has declared that it would not join the BRI[11] Instead, the EU launched its own connectivity strategy with Asia (EU Joint Communication, 2018; European Commission, 2019: 5) and, more recently, signed an infrastructure deal with Japan for connectivity between Europe and Asia, an agreement described as a rival and riposte to China's BRI (Skala-Kuhmann, 2019; Eva, 2019; EU & Japan, 2019). Additionally, the EU has recently established a regulatory scheme to screen foreign direct investment in the EU by state-owned enterprises.[12] Most critically, the EU has now labelled China 'an economic competitor in the pursuit of technological leadership, and a systemic rival promoting alternative models of governance'.[13] There are in fact many more competing schemes against the BRI at the moment and,[14] no doubt many more will emerge.

2.2 The BRI Born as a Geopolitical Strategy

The objections to the BRI from major developed countries lie in the fact that it is perceived by Western countries that the BRI is part of China's geopolitical and geo-economic play at a global scale.[15] To understand the nature of the BRI, we must first uncover the underlying reasons for its development and the background to the birth of the BRI. These factors have effectively determined the initial perception of the Initiative as a geopolitical move, and that this perception has increasingly led to a view that the practice of the BRI and some other recent trade-related conduct of China as Chinese geo-economic manoeuvring.

11 For some time, there were uncertainties as to whether the EU would join China's BRI. See Bohman, Mardell, & Roming, 2018. In April 2019, EU officials formally confirmed that the EU as a bloc would not consider joining the Initiative (though individual countries are free to do so, as Hungary, Poland, Bulgaria, Greece, Portugal and Italy have done). See Valero, 2019.

12 According to the European Commission, the new scheme establishing a framework for screening foreign direct investment entered into force in April 2019 and was fully applied from November 2020. It focuses on foreign investment in critical assets, technologies and infrastructure. See European Commission, 2019: 10. Although nothing is said about investment from China, few would be under any illusion that the scheme does not have Chinese investment in mind. See van Leeuwen, 2018.

13 The EU does acknowledge, at the same time, that in some areas China is its cooperation partner and in other areas a negotiating partner. See European Commission, 2019.

14 For the various schemes, see Competing Visions, 2019; World Bank, 2019: 46–47; Morris, 2020.

15 Indeed, many scholars have insisted that the BRI must be understood as a global geopolitical and geo-economic strategy. See Carrai, Defraigne, & Wouters, 2020: 3.

There are several critical factors in the background in which China's global investment strategy, expressed in the BRI, emerged. Obviously, China's growing economic power is an important factor, and so are the reform frustration and disillusion over the post-War 'international economic order' among many countries that include China. Most importantly, however, is China's confidence with its own 'governance model' and its demand for a leadership role in international governance. In a broader context, the emergence of the BRI is also derived from China's frustration in the RTAs movement that saw China being excluded in some major RTA negotiations.

As discussed in Chapter 2, China played only very limited roles in the efforts to establish a New International Economic Order (NIEO). In Chapter 3, we then began to see the major development of regional – in contrast to multilateral – trade agreements (RTAs), which soon became a geopolitical contest between the existing and rising powers as well as creating divisions among nations along ideological lines.

By the time the development of RTAs became a significant geopolitical contest, China had also become a major economic and trading power. It is important to acknowledge the fact that, by the turn of the 21st century, the growth of China's outward investment effectively became inevitable as a result of its growing economic power, and necessary as a result of its growing foreign exchange reserve.[16] While China continues to maintain certain barriers to trade and inward foreign investment (though many of which are allowed under the WTO negotiation agreements on China's membership), China was also looking abroad for economic opportunities and thus for trade and investment liberalisation.

It was at this conjunction, between the development of RTAs and China's growing economic power, that the 'super' RTAs began to emerge, with two elements that were particularly crucial: participants in the 'super' RTAs effectively rewrite trade and investment rules and there was an 'Anyone-but-China' (ABC) approach to forming such agreements. Not surprisingly, among the various proposed 'super' RTAs China was only participating in the negotiation of the RCEP, which is largely Asia-focused.

Understandably, Chinese policymakers considered such agreements as the TPP 'a force that could rip apart the regional economic integration of East Asia' (Song & Wen, 2012: 107). In their opinion, and also in light of the negotiation of the TTIP, the TPP was seen as nothing but 'a tool to economically contain China's rise' (People's Daily, 2013: 6; Song & Wen,

16 See the charts on GDP and Foreign Reserve in Chen, 2016a: 867. Of course, adding to these two factors was the overcapacity in China as a result of an investment-led development strategy.

2012: 107).[17] Sceptical scholars then viewed the TPP as the geopolitical medium for the United States' return to the region and a front for a 'soft confrontation' with China (Song & Wen, 2012: 109).[18] A prominent China trade policy expert expresses this view thus:

> The rise of China's economic power and the strengthening of East Asian economy have broken the existing global trade structures. Western powers now intend, through the negotiations of TPP and TTIP, to rewrite trade rules and regain their leadership powers in international trade. By doing so, Western powers will share the economic prosperity while also contain the ever increasing influence of China.
>
> (People's Daily, 2013: 6)

These Chinese suspicions were soon emphatically confirmed when the then US President Barack Obama declared in 2016:

> As a Pacific power, the United States has pushed to develop a high-standard Trans-Pacific Partnership, a trade deal that puts American workers first and makes sure we write the rules of the road for trade in the 21st century . . . America should write the rules. America should call the shots. Other countries should play by the rules that America and our partners set, and not the other way around . . . The United States, not countries like China, should write [the rules].
>
> (Obama, 2016)

Clearly, while economic powers and interests still work in the background in support of claims for regional leadership, the global geopolitical rivalry is the actual force that almost impels the existing powers and rising powers into a showdown in the efforts of the rising powers to establish a new international economic order. This showdown has threatened to disintegrate the existing multilateral order established under the auspices of the Bretton Woods system. It is also in this context that it was reported that President Xi said at the Peripheral Diplomacy Work Conference in October 2013: 'We must build the Silk Road Economic Belt and 21st Century Maritime Silk Road, creating a new regional economic order' (Cai, 2017: 3). Seeing the BRI as China's response to the TPP, it is claimed that there is 'a fundamental competitive tension around the question of whether China or the United

17 For further analysis on the Chinese position regarding the TPP, see Mulgan, 2013.
18 It is noteworthy that China did, at one stage, consider joining the TPP.

States will ultimately determine the rules for trade and investment in the region' (Meltzer, 2017).

The BRI thus emerged at a time when China perceived a need and possibility to take a proactive approach to international relations in responding to the geopolitical repositioning and rebalancing of global powers at the time, believing that there is an international consensus that it is China's turn to shape the international order (Wang, 2018: 241–242),[19] or that it is time for China to promote new multilateral institutions that follow China's norms and principles (Yuan, 2019: 95).

The BRI, together with the Asian Infrastructure Investment Bank (AIIB) and other 'going out' strategies, was consequently widely perceived as a Chinese geopolitical strategy that demands the repositioning and rebalancing of international powers,[20] especially between the rising and 'super' powers.[21] Such a perception is then reinforced, from time to time, by the Chinese media, such as the *Xinhua News Agency*, and by Chinese academics. Thus, *Xinhua* stressed that the BRI is in fact a Chinese geopolitical strategy (Xinhua, 2015a, 2015b; Hu, 2015). To hail the BRI as the gift of 'Chinese wisdom' or 'project of the century' (The Economist, 2018b), and assert that the BRI is part of China's global governance push or Chinese renaissance scheme (China Think Tank, 2017; Yuan, 2019: 96–99), would hardly help to allay concerns over the scheme in many countries. Some Chinese scholars went so far as to claim that the BRI is an avenue to a 'post Westphalian world', which of course is to be interpreted as a fundamental challenge to the current global political and economic status quo (Wade, 2018). Most recently, a prominent Chinese scholar specialising in the BRI and a member of a Chinese government think tank, claimed that the BRI has three principal objectives: to internationalise the *Renminbi*, to establish a China-dominated market to rival the American and European-dominated markets, and to establish a new regional international economic order that would raise the right to speak on issues concerning the international economic order, although it would not overthrow the international order led by the US (Lu, 2019). As such, it was almost inevitable that the BRI became

19 There are also scholars who believe that we are now entering a new phase of globalisation led by China and driven by the BRI. See Gao, 2018: 326–328; Li, 2019: 3.

20 Thus, the aim of the BRI is described as 'to extricate China from its strategic encirclement by the US and its allies, while opening up further trade and investment opportunities for Chinese capitalism.' See Symonds, 2015. Similarly, Australian Foreign Minister Julie Bishop described the BRI as China's vehicle for greater political and strategic influence in the region. See Wroe, 2018a; Leverett & Wu, 2016: 110–132.

21 See discussions in Chapter 3 previously.

not only controversial but also a point of contention between China and the US and its allies.

3. Geo-Economic Manoeuvring

While 'geopolitical strategy' or 'geopolitical rivalry' are the terms being frequently applied in analysing the BRI, another notion, the recently emerged term, 'geo-economics' is also being used (see Global Agenda Councils, 2015; Stiglitz, 2016; Blackwill & Harris, 2016; Golley & Ingle, 2018: 42–59; Wigell & Vihma, 2016; Scholvin & Wigell, 2018), and has become increasingly popular in the explicit or implicit analysis of the BRI. More recently and pointedly, 'economic coercion' is often used to describe China's reaction to political disagreements from smaller countries such as, most notably, Norway, South Korea, Australia and Lithuania (Zhang, 2018; Wiśniewski, 2021; Blumenthal, 2018; Chen, 2019; Uren, 2020).

Geo-economics, as a notion, emerged in the early 1990s. While it has been widely used as a term to describe power politics by economic means, or 'war by other means' (Blackwill & Harris, 2016), its meaning is not precisely defined (Scholvin & Wigell, 2018). It is sometimes seen as a subvariant of geopolitics.[22] However, at least in its early usage, it envisages a geopolitical strategy in which capital replaces firepower, civilian innovation replaces military advancement, and markets replace garrisons and military bases (Scholvin & Wigell, 2018: 5). Based on this understanding, geo-economics is defined as 'the use of economic instruments to promote and defend national interests and to produce geopolitical results; and the effects of another nation's economic actions on a country's geopolitical goals' (Blackwill & Harris, 2016: 20; Scholvin & Wigell, 2018). In other words, it implies the advancement of the geostrategic goals of one party, and is not seen as a mutually beneficial relationship (Wigell & Vihma, 2016: 606).

Although not always expressed in the explicit language of actually accusing China of practising inequality or imposing a new form of colonialism,[23] many of the criticisms towards the BRI as a geo-economic strategy are in fact criticisms of such a nature (Li, 2020). Thus, among the many criticisms of the BRI practice, it is accused of being a means of domination by China (Hsu, 2017);[24] exporting a Chinese state-led development model (Perlez &

22 In fact, neither is the term 'geopolitics' precisely defined. Suffice it to say, for the purpose of our discussion, geopolitics is primarily about 'understanding politics based on considerations of location and physical geography'. See Scholvin, 2016: 13.

23 In some specific context, such accusation has indeed been made. See Li, 2019: 8. For a detailed analysis of the various accusation, concerns and criticisms, see Wang, 2018.

24 This is explicitly stated by China's own media, see e.g., Five Years of BRI, 2018.

Huang, 2017); lacking genuine benefits for local communities (The Economist, 2018b); setting up projects against public opposition,[25] objections over labour policies or concerns over national security (Kynge, 2018); being developmentally unsustainable (Financial Times Opinion, 2018; Rogin, 2018); targeting mainly poorer countries and employing a 'debt-trap strategy' (Fernando & Chang, 2018);[26] creating new markets and safeguarding access to raw materials for China (EU Ambassadors, 2018); and involving other Sino-centric practices. These criticisms of the BRI ultimately led to backlash against the BRI in countries like Malaysia, Sri Lanka and Pakistan (Rogin, 2018, Wang, 2018).

More directly on the use of geo-economic power, it has been asserted that 'Mr Xi is aiming to use China's wealth and industrial know-how to create a new kind of globalisation that will dispense with the rules of the aging Western-dominated institutions. The goal is to refashion the global economic order, drawing countries and companies more tightly into China's orbit' (Perlez & Huang, 2017). Others have put it more explicitly: 'China has been utilizing the economic tools at her disposal, such as trade, investment and finance in order to project power abroad and advance China's geopolitical objectives' (Pathirana, 2018: 123). Not surprisingly, some have simply accused China as being 'the world's leading practitioner of geo-economics' (Blackwill & Harris, 2016: 11).

4. Global Governance: Reform or Rejection

China, after facing the various criticisms, questions, misgivings and resistance, and after six years of implementation and experience of the BRI, has finally begun to respond to some of the concerns (Xi, 2019; BRI Five Years, 2019).[27] Thus, China has recently begun to emphasise the needs of local communities, economic and environmental sustainability, and mutual understanding among all parties and people involved in BRI projects

25 An often-cited example is the Ituango dam in Colombia, which was strongly opposed by local communities, but went ahead and later, in 2018, caused the evacuation of 26,000 people due to a landslide. See Kynge, 2018.

26 It is claimed that two-thirds of countries involved in the BRI have debt ratings below investment grade. See Bowen, 2016: 12. More specifically, it is recently claimed that 27 BRI countries' sovereign debt is regarded as 'junk' by the three main ratings agencies and another 14 have no rating at all. See Greer, 2018. On the other hand, a recent report in relation to the BRI in the Pacific has concluded that China has not practiced debt diplomacy. See Rajah, Dayant, & Pryke, 2019.

27 Not very long ago, China seemed to simply ignore the criticisms, regarding them as Western refusal to accept China's rise. See Balding, 2018.

(Wang & Chen, 2020). Also, as part of efforts to respond to criticisms, China pledged in September 2018 to waive debts for the least-developed African countries provided they maintain diplomatic ties with China (Needham, 2018).[28] Because of these efforts, there is now a talk of 'BRI 2.0' (Ang, 2019; Wang & Chen, 2020).

However, at the heart of these misgivings over the BRI is the lack of trust and confidence caused by the particular approach taken by China to the implementation of the Initiative, an approach that reinforces the perception of the BRI as geopolitical and geo-economic manoeuvring. Put simply, the Chinese approach is typically a relational approach that is largely bilateral and relies on soft law (i.e., non-binding memoranda of understanding) (Wang, 2019).[29] The BRI lacks a crucial element heavily emphasised by Western nations: that is, the rule of law (Wang, 2019: 223). Unlike the Asian Infrastructure Investment Bank, there is no institutional framework nor clearly set principles that would be applied to all parties or projects included in the BRI projects. Indeed, there is not even a clearly defined notion of BRI or a clear geographical coverage or types of activities or projects covered by the BRI.[30] The non-binding, and often kept confidential, memoranda of understanding, the effect of which is described as a gesture of 'engaging but not endorsing' (Okano-Heijmans & Kamo, 2019), are in most cases vague commitments to cooperate from individual countries on a bilateral basis.[31] Such an approach can easily be seen as China-centric geopolitical and geo-economic plays with, in most cases, weaker partners.

More importantly, such an approach by China is not likely to be received well in Western countries, where the promotion of liberal market economies, as well as sustainability, maintenance of open and transparent process through the rule of law and the protection of democracy and human rights,[32] are all relevant and valid considerations for trade and investment policy-making. Thus, one of the reasons the EU changed its mind about

28 In fact, China had been renegotiating debts with many poor countries for many years, often resulting in new terms in favour of the borrowing countries. See Lratz, Feng, & Wright, 2019.

29 In addition to the specific MoUs for the BRI, China has also signed a large number of the various strategic partnership agreements with most countries involved in the BRI. See Yuan, 2019: 100–101.

30 The BRI thus becomes an 'umbrella project', see Hart-Landsberg, 2018. Chinese scholars too have argued that the BRI needs to have some clear objectives and its scope needs to be narrowed down. See Lu, 2019.

31 For an interesting comparison of differences in the different memoranda of understanding, see Wang, 2019: 226–228.

32 For a short but reasonably concise description of the establishment of the present international order, see Wang, 2018: 228–235; Haass, 2017.

engaging with the BRI was, it is said, because that 'truly multilateral cooperation fora and dialogues are missing' (Amighini, 2018). The present Chinese practice is then described thus: 'It is multilateral in aspirational form, but bilateral in function and content,' in the absence of any overarching international framework (Sussex & Clarke, 2017; Skala-Kuhmann, 2019). Such a bilateral structure for cooperation in the BRI is seen in Europe as leading 'to unequal distribution of powers which China exploits' and that China was trying to divide Europe (EU Ambassadors, 2018),[33] to challenge EU cohesion and to undermine European standards (Bohman, Mardell, & Roming, 2018). In the same vein it is claimed that '[s]ome Asian countries, including India and Vietnam, are wary [of the BRI] and most Western countries share their unease' because of the particular approach taken by China (The Economist, 2018b). Thus, US Defence Secretary James Mattis said in 2018 that: 'No one nation should put itself into a position of dictating [the BRI]'. It is further claimed that in January 2018 French President Emmanuel Macron warned that the BRI 'cannot be the road of a new hegemony that will make the countries they traverse into vassal states' (The Economist, 2018b). A diplomat recently commented that 'what China wants is really vague rules, and the right to interpret them' (The Economist, 2018a). It is also asserted that, though '[r]arely mounting direct challenges, China has instead tested, probed and introduced ambiguities into every aspect of global governance' (The Economist, 2018a). In short, China is perceived as not working with the existing international rules under a multilateral framework, nor endeavouring to reform global governance, instead, China is seen as trying to create a new international economic order of its own design.

China's new 'design', however, lacks clarity, certainty and consistency, as far as the implementation of the BRI is concerned (Wang & Rosenau, 2009; Mazarr, Heath, & Cevallos, 2018; Hart & Johnson, 2019; Cohen, 2019; Pathirana, 2018). Until quite recently, it could be said that China had not challenged the Western-originated multilateral framework nor has it had any clear or comprehensive plan to replace the existing system with a China-led system (Cohen, 2019: 124). China did, however, demand a larger share of policy-making powers and, like many other super powers, has been selective in complying with international norms. More recently, China has, on many occasions, become assertive and even aggressive in certain areas

33 In this regard, while China uses the'16+1' (16 Central and East European (CEE) states and China) as an example of its multilateralism (see Para 2 (1) of BRI Five Years, 2019), it was often criticised as a means to divide Europe (see Kavalski & Mayer, 2019). The 16 countries include Bulgaria, the Czech Republic, Croatia, Estonia, Hungary, Latvia, Lithuania, Poland, Romania, Slovakia, Slovenia, Albania, Macedonia, Montenegro, Serbia and Bosnia.

of international tension, such as in its responses to criticisms on its practice in the South China Sea. In its most recent policy statement on international relations and global governance (White Paper, 2019), China continues its rhetoric about establishing a human community of shared destiny (*renlei mingyun gongtongti*) and a new type of international relations, as well as the promotion of economic globalisation (Li, 2016; Chi, 2019; Huang, 2019). Here, China is trying to use the notion of 'community of shared destiny' to offer an alternative vision of international relations and, hence, a different world view and a different set of values (Yuan, 2019: 108). At the same time, China nevertheless makes it clear that it supports multilateralism and an international system centred around the United Nations. In its argument for reform of global governance, it focuses on the reform of the UN, the IMF, the World Bank and the WTO. It seems that China's position is to reform the existing multilateral institutions and their governance by incorporating China's world view and values.

However, the Chinese approach to multilateralism has been hardly consistent; its practice, especially in relation to the implementation of BRI as just discussed, remains fundamentally bilateral in nature. Not surprisingly, China's behaviour in multilateralism is described as such:

> China has expressed its commitment to a fair and equitable global governance model. At the same time, China's engagement in favour of multilateralism is sometimes selective and based on a different understanding of the rules-based international order. While China has often repeated its legitimate request for reforming global governance to give greater participation and decision-making power to emerging economies, it has not always been willing to accept new rules reflecting the responsibility and accountability that come with its increased role. Selectively upholding some norms at the expense of others weakens the sustainability of the rules-based international order.
>
> (European Commission, 2019: 2)

Indeed, China has so far offered its critics more rhetorical assurance than specific policy or practice. It is reported that President Xi Jinping has recently stated that the BRI is 'neither the post-World War II Marshall Plan, nor is it a Chinese conspiracy' (Suokas, 2018). He is also reported to have insisted that China has no intention of playing 'self-serving geopolitical games' (EU Ambassadors, 2018). Official government documents also explicitly declare that the BRI is not about establishing a geopolitical nor a military alliance (BRI Five Years, 2019). Also recently, both Chinese President Xi Jinping and Chinese Foreign Minister Wang Yi declared that the BRI would respect international rules and that they would be applied according to market rules (Xi, 2019b; Cainey, 2018). Yet, neither the 2019 White Paper nor China's official five-year report on the BRI explains how China's largest ever strategic project (that is, the BRI) might work under the existing multilateral framework or what international law and rules might be applied to its implementation.[34] On the other hand, as mentioned previously, China, in the last few years, has not even bothered to hide its economic bullying of countries with which it has political disagreements. This 'bullying' amounts to not only breaching international norms, but is also in total disregard of bilateral, regional and multilateral rules on dispute resolution.[35]

Not surprisingly, Chinese academics have offered very little commentary/literature to explain how the BRI might work under any new institutional arrangements or within the existing multilateral framework. As mentioned previously, there have been some Chinese arguments for establishing a new type of international relations in the name of establishing a human community of shared destiny. There has been, however, very little substance in the arguments. Further, there are suggestions that China might use bilateralism as stepping-stone and eventually form a regional or even multilateral arrangement based on the various bilateral free trade agreements (Klett & Oswald, 2018: 75–93; Shi, 2018: 9–31). Other scholars have examined the compatibility of the BRI cooperation with the existing trade agreements and concluded that a new type of agreement would be required (Lee, 2018: 59–80). Many have focused on specific mechanisms, especially on dispute resolution (Tao & Zhong, 2018; Jiang, 2018: 59–80; Xiong & Tomasic, 2019). Whatever the suggestions that have been discussed, there is not yet a concrete suggestion that would bring trade and investment into one scheme and take into consideration both international rules and institutional arrangements.

China's rise should lead to reform – not rejection – of existing global governance, a task for those genuinely wanting economic integration for the greater good (Stiglitz, 2016). So far, China has not demonstrated, especially at a practical level, strong advocacy of global governance reforms.

34 During the Second Belt and Road Forum for International Cooperation in 2019, Xi Jinping delivered a speech at a press conference on 27 April 2019. At the press conference, Xi suggests that the Belt and Road Forum for International Cooperation should be established as a regularly convened multilateral platform that would serve as a framework for multilateral cooperation. Xi did not however elaborate how it might work and whether he has any intention to establish this Forum as an institutional structure. See Xi, 2019a.

35 These issues are discussions in Chapter 5.

5. The Greatest Challenge Yet: State Capitalism and the Rise of Protectionism

Whatever the measures of reform and opening-up policies that have been implemented in China since 1978, there is little doubt that the Chinese economy is a state-led and controlled one (Chen, 2016a: Ch 18 & 19), or more precisely a Party-controlled economy (Chen, 2016b, 2020). The BRI is, as discussed previously, clearly a Party/State project that is both planned, coordinated and implemented by the State, not by market forces. Though there is hardly, at the moment, any distinction between the State and the Party in China, for purpose of convenience, we refer to the Chinese economy and the BRI as state capitalism.

Just as China, as a rising power backed by its economic power of the state capitalism that is historically unprecedented in modern history, poses a credible challenge to the liberal economic order established after WWII, the West, but especially the US, has begun to retreat from this established order. The Chinese challenge and the West and US retreat from the post WWII liberal economic order means that the world liberal economic order is facing its greatest ever challenge.

When the 2008 global financial crisis (GFC) landed in the US and quickly spread to other countries, the G7[36] – the very core force supporting the liberal economic order – was clearly not strong enough to contain the crisis and, hence, the first ever G20 summit was convened to fight against it.[37] The G20 is not just an institution composed of G7 and emerging economies; it includes members with some entirely different politico-economic systems. More important than the differences between the G20 member states were the measures taken by all these countries to combat the impacts of the GFC which were in every sense against the liberal economic order ideology. This is because the principal measure taken was to inject trillions of dollars of public money to effectively transfer private debts into the public sector and to bail out private firms which were in financial stress.[38]

36 Its membership includes Canada, France, Germany, Italy, Japan, the UK and the United States.

37 The G20 membership includes Argentina, Australia, Brazil, Canada, China, France, Germany, India, Indonesia, Italy, Japan, Republic of Korea, Mexico, Russia, Saudi Arabia, South Africa, Turkey, the United Kingdom, the United States and the European Union. Although formed as a financial ministers' meeting in 1999, its first ever heads of government summit was only convened in 2008, specifically to address the GFC.

38 There is no shortage of literature on the origins of and responses to the 2008 GFC, see eg Ramskogler, 2014; Wray, 2012.

Just when the impacts of the GFC had begun to be addressed, with its underlying problems far from being resolved (The McKinsey Global Institute, 2018), the populist Trump was elected US President and took office in 2017. Trump's 'America First' foreign policy did not only impose unilateral actions against his perceived 'enemies' (such as tariffs against China), but also took offensive actions against traditional allies (such as tariffs against the EU, the renegotiations of North America Free Trade Agreement (NAFTA), and the withdrawal from TPP). The Trump administration was no friend to the WTO, free trade nor indeed to the liberal economic order. Globalisation was in retreat and 'deglobalisation' gained currency during Trump's administration.

If the populist 'America First' policy was to end after the election of Biden in 2020 (who took office in 2021), another global crisis was soon to strike much harder at the liberal economic order. A once-in-a-century global health crisis – the Covid-19 pandemic – emerged towards the end of 2019 with its severe health and economic impact continues until this day. Government responses to it, almost universally, have revealed the weaknesses and downsides of, and challenged many assumptions for, free trade and investment as the cornerstone of the liberal economic order. In order to deal with the impacts of Covid, governments were not just injecting massive amount of money, mostly borrowed, into their economies; they were bailing out all kinds of companies and firms as well as supporting private employment.[39] Facing the shortage of health protective equipment and Covid-19 vaccines and medicine, export controls were soon imposed by many countries, openly or covertly.[40] Coupled with the lingering 'America First' ideology, 'decoupling from China' took hold in popular and academic discourse (Rapoz, 2020; Witt, 2020; Rudd, 2019), and much worse, it has now become a rapidly growing concern.[41] Finally, when supply chains were interrupted by the continuation of the Covid-19 pandemic, which also caused major inflation in many countries, diversification of supply chains and deglobalisation has now become fashionable, with many countries actively encouraging the 're-shoring' or 'friend shoring' of manufacturing (see e.g. Japan

39 There are a number of databases that recorded governments' responses to Covid-19 and, among them, the following are some precise summaries of these responses: Oxford Covid-19; the World Bank Covid-19; the ILO Covid-19.

40 On international trade and Covid-19 including export control, see WTO Covid-19. On specific measure imposed by various countries, see WTO Covid-19 Trade.

41 For good analyses on the origin and trends of 'decoupling' in the recent years, see China Center, 2021; EU Chamber of Commerce in China and MERICS, 2021; Cerdeiro et al., 2021; BATEMAN, 2022.

Relocation, 2020).[42] Most recently, the Indo-Pacific Economic Framework (IPEF) (as discussed in Chapter 3) and the China Strategy of the US (China Strategy, 2022), issued around the same time of the IPEF, have now firmly placed geopolitical struggles on trade and investment agenda. What has not been considered is that all these reactions and responses, not driven by markets but by governments, are diametrically opposed to the liberal economic ideology that many of these countries wish to uphold.

Various industrial reports, as just mentioned, have warned of the high costs of 'decoupling'. It is thus difficult to predict the future of 'decoupling' or, for that matter, diversification of supply chains. It is, however, clear that state capitalism practiced by China and the 'deglobalisation' ('decoupling' or diversification) trends now represent the greatest challenge to the liberal international economic order ever since its embodiment in the international economic governance and its structure.

6. Conclusion

There is nothing wrong if the BRI has a geopolitical dimension, and it is not unreasonable either that emerging powers demand a greater share of power with the existing powers. The critical question is whether a rising power like China would be content to work within and with the existing multilateral framework that was founded on liberal economic ideology. In other words, it is critical to question and examine whether China will be a contributor, not a challenger, to the reform of global governance and development of international law. This choice, by China, will also decide whether there will be a race to hegemony[43] or whether there will be an evolving accommodation of rising powers.

Our world, and the globalisation and regulation of it, is multifaceted and multidimensional. It does not need to consist of simple dichotomies such as conflict and cooperation, control and resistance, norm and power, and participation and competition. Leadership does not necessarily mean the creating of a new regime, nor does geopolitical rebalancing and repositioning necessitate the writing of entirely new rules. The world is complicated, yet also sufficiently sophisticated, to be able to accommodate emerging powers and to allow emerging powers to work within existing rules, albeit

42 It is now almost universal that political parties in Western countries would advocate the 're-shoring' or 'friend shoring' of manufacturing during election campaigns.

43 For analyses on how the emerging economies in Asia have come to compete economically and politically with the United States, see generally de Silva, 2009: 34–72; Ramirez, 2006: 17; Jacques, 2009; White, 2013.

with reforms and changes. The critical question then becomes; is our existing global governance regime capable of resolving conflicts and disputes among participants, but especially major powers, in the existing multilateral forums?

References

Amighini, Alessia (2018), 'Need for improved EU-China relations in the belt and road era', *International Affairs*, 31 July, available at www.internationalaffairs.org.au/australianoutlook/improved-eu-china-relations-belt-road-era/ (last accessed 2/8/18).

Ang, Yuen Yuen (2019), 'Demystifying belt and road: The struggle to define China's "project of the century"', *Foreign Affairs*, 22 May, available at www.foreignaffairs.com/articles/china/2019-05-22/demystifying-belt-and-road (last accessed 23/5/19).

Arha, Kaush (2021), 'A hidden key to the G7's infrastructure ambitions: Blue dot network', *Atlantic Council*, 12 June, available at www.atlanticcouncil.org/blogs/new-atlanticist/a-hidden-key-to-the-g7s-infrastructure-ambitions-blue-dot-network/ (last accessed 2/5/22).

Balding, Christopher (2018), 'Why democracies are turning against belt and road', *Foreign Affairs*, 24 October, available at www.foreignaffairs.com/articles/china/2018-10-24/why-democracies-are-turning-against-belt-and-road?from=groupmessage&isappinstalled=0 (last accessed 31/10/18).

Bateman, Jon (2022), *U.S-China Technological "Decoupling": A Strategy and Policy Framework* (Carnegie Endowment for International Peace), available at https://carnegieendowment.org/2022/04/25/u.s.-china-technological-decoupling-strategy-and-policy-framework-pub-86897 (last accessed 8/5/22).

Blackwill, Robert & Harris, Jennifer (2016), W*ar by Other Means: Geoeconomics and Statecraft* (Cambridge, MA: Belknap Press).

Blumenthal, Dan (2018), 'Economic coercion as a tool in China's grand strategy', 24 July, available at www.foreign.senate.gov/imo/media/doc/072418_Blumenthal_Testimony.pdf (last accessed 5/4/22).

Bohman, Viking, Mardell, Jacob & Roming, Tatjana (2018), 'Responding to China's belt and road initiative: Two steps for a European strategy', 26 June, available at www.merics.org/en/blog/responding-chinas-belt-and-road-initiative-two-steps-european-strategy (last accessed 2/8/18).

Bowen, James (2016), 'Too big to ignore: Assessing the strategic implications of China's belt and road initiative', Being a special report of the Australian Strategic Policy Institute, Canberra, August.

BRI Country List (2022), 'A list of countries that have signed agreements for BRI', available at www.yidaiyilu.gov.cn/xwzx/roll/77298.htm (last accessed 1/5/22).

BRI Five Years (2019), 'The belt and road initiative progress, contributions and prospects', official (five-year) report released by the Office of the Leading Group for Promoting the Belt and Road Initiative. An English version is available at https://eng.yidaiyilu.gov.cn/zchj/qwfb/86739.htm (last accessed 26/4/19).

Cai, Peter (2017), *Understanding China's Belt and Road Initiative* (Sydney: Lowy Institute for International Policy).

Cainey, Andrew (2018), 'Belt and road is not a (completely) closed ship', *Chatham House*, available at www.chathamhouse.org/expert/comment/belt-and-road-not-completely-closed-shop?gclid=EAIaIQobChMIsLqp5IPf3AIVzaqWCh22ega0EAMYASAAEgKh-fD_BwE (last accessed 9/8/18).

Carrai, M. A., Defraigne, J. & Wouters, J. (2020), 'The belt and road initiative and global governance: by way of introduction, in Carrai, Defraigne & Wouters, 2020.

Carrai, M. A., Defraigne, J. & Wouters, J. (eds.) (2020), *The Belt and Road Initiative and Global Governance*, (Cheltenham, UK: Edward Elgar Publishing Limited).

Cerdeiro, Diego A, Eugster, Johannes, Rui, C. Mano, Muir, Dirk & Peiris, Shanaka J. (2021), 'Sizing Up the effects of technological decoupling', IMF Working Paper WP/21/69, available at www.imf.org/en/Publications/WP/Issues/2021/03/12/Sizing-Up-the-Effects-of-Technological-Decoupling-50125 (last accessed 8/5/22).

Chen, Duanjie (2019), 'Countering coercion China's economic: No fear but resolve, no illusion but diversification', Canadian Public Policy, available at https://macdonaldlaurier.ca/files/pdf/20190827_China_Economic_Coercion_Chen_PAPER_FWeb.pdf (last accessed 5/4/22).

Chen, Jianfu (2016a), *Chinese Law: Context and Transformation*, Revised and Expanded Edition (Leiden/London: Brill Nijhoff).

Chen, Jianfu (2016b), 'Out of the shadows and back to the future: CPC and law in China', 24 (2) *Asia Pacific Law Review* 176.

Chen, Jianfu (2020), 'Chinese law & legal reform: Where to from here', 50 (1) *HKLJ* 243.

Chi, He (2019), 'To establish a right to speak in international law for the one belt and one road initiative: A perspective from the supply of public goods', 6 *Research in International Law* (*Guoji Fa Yanjiu*) 63.

China Center, US Chamber of Commerce (2021), 'Understanding decoupling: Macro trends and industry impacts', available at www.uschamber.com/assets/archived/images/024001_us_china_decoupling_report_fin.pdf (last accessed 8/5/22).

China Strategy (2022), 'The administration's approach to the people's republic of China', Speech by Anthony J. Blinken, Secretary of State, 26 May 2022, available at www.state.gov/the-administrations-approach-to-the-peoples-republic-of-china/ (last accessed 27/5/22).

China Think Tank (2017), 'The global governance ideas of secretary general Xi Jinping', *China Think Tank Net*, 23 July 2017, available at https://mp.weixin.qq.com/s/6LVqh6_D4KPe4fCIZdLvLQ (last accessed 3/8/18).

CNBC (2018), 'Australia, Japan join US infrastructure push in Asia', 31 July 2018, available at www.cnbc.com/2018/07/31/australia-japan-join-us-infrastructure-push-in-asia.html (last accessed 31/7/18).

Cohen, Jerome A. (2019), 'Law and power in China's international relations', 52 *NYU Journal of International Law and Politics* 123.

Commonwealth (2013), 'Mapping the terrain: Strengthening commonwealth economic cooperation: Potential implications of the Trans-Pacific Partnership (TPP) and the Regional Economic Cooperation Partnership (RCEP) free trade agreement on commonwealth small states and LDC', available at http://secretariat.thecommonwealth.org/job/191203/167709/257297/ead_pbcwg_0664.htm (last accessed 21/12/13).

Competing Visions (2019), 'Competing visions', *Reconnecting Asia*, Center for Strategic and International Studies (CSIS), available at https://reconnectingasia.csis.org/analysis/competing-visions/ (last accessed 20/4/19).

Corre, Philippe Le (2017), 'Europe's mixed views on China's one belt, one road initiative', 23 May 2017, available at www.brookings.edu/blog/order-from-chaos/2017/05/23/europes-mixed-views-on-chinas-one-belt-one-road-initiative/ (last accessed 3/8/18).

Daly, Nadia (2017), 'One belt one road: NT business welcome Chinese investment despite reluctance over "new silk road"', *ABC News*, 9 August 2017, available at www.abc.net.au/news/2017-08-08/one-belt-one-road-nt-businesses-welcome-chinese-investment/8783846 (last accessed 7/8/18).

de Silva, Dharma (2009), 'Building BRICKS of the new global economy, competition and trading system', 14 (4) *Sri Lankan Journal of Management* 34.

Deepak, B. R. (ed.) (2018), *China's Global Rebalancing and the New Silk Road* (Singapore: Springer Nature Singapore Pte Ltd).

Divided Europe (2019), 'Divided Europe faces China belt and road test', *The Business Times*, 25 April 2019, available at www.businesstimes.com.sg/government-economy/divided-europe-faces-china-belt-and-road-test (last accessed 15/10/19).

Dossani, Rafiq, Bouey, Jennifer & Zhu, Keren (2020), 'Demystifying the belt and road initiative: A clarification of its key features, objectives and impacts', *Rand, WR-1338*, May 2020, available at www.rand.org/pubs/working_papers/WR1338.html (last accessed 1/5/22).

The Economist (2018a), 'Xi's world order: July 2024', *The Economist*, 7 July, available at www.economist.com/the-world-if/2018/07/07/xis-world-order-july-2024 (last accessed 7/8/18).

The Economist (2018b), 'China belt and road plans are to be welcomed and worried about', *The Economist*, 26 July, available at *www.economist.com/leaders/2018/07/26/chinas-belt-and-road-plans-are-to-be-welcomed-and-worried-about* (last accessed 29/7/18).

EU Ambassadors (2018), 'EU ambassadors band together against silk road', April, available at https://thediplomat.com/2018/04/eu-ambassadors-condemn-chinas-belt-and-road-initiative/ (last accessed 22/7/18).

EU Chamber of Commerce in China and MERICS (2021), 'Decoupling: Severed ties and patchwork globalisation', available at https://merics.org/en/report/decoupling-severed-ties-and-patchwork-globalisation (last accessed 8/5/22).

EU & Japan (2019), 'EU Japan take on China's BRI with own silk road', 4 October 2019, available at www.dw.com/en/eu-japan-take-on-chinas-bri-with-own-silk-road/a-50697761 (last accessed 15/10/19).

EU Joint Communication (2018), 'Joint communication to the European parliament, the council, the European economic and social committee', The Committee of the Regions and the European Investment Bank on Connecting Europe and Asia – Building Blocks for an EU Strategy, JOIN(2018) 31, 19.09.2018.

European Commission (2019), 'EU-China – A strategic outlook', 12 March 2019, at 1. An English text is available at https://ec.europa.eu/commission/sites/beta-political/files/communication-eu-china-a-strategic-outlook.pdf (last accessed 15/10/19).

Eva, Joanna (2019), 'Japan and the EU sign infrastructure deal to rival China's belt and road', *European Views*, 30 September 2019, available at www.european-views.com/2019/09/japan-and-the-eu-sign-infrastructure-deal-to-rival-chinas-belt-and-road/ (last accessed 15/10/19).

Fang, Frank (2018), 'Russian media is harshly critical of China's "one belt, one road" projects in Eurasia', *Epoch Times*, 8 August, available at www.theepoch times.com/russian-media-harshly-criticizes-chinas-one-belt-one-road-projects-in-eurasia_2618886.html (last accessed 9/8/18).

Fernando, Gavin & Chang, Charis (2018), 'The story China went to furious length to stop from airing', 23 June, available at www.news.com.au/finance/economy/world-economy/the-story-china-went-to-furious-lengths-to-stop-from-airing/news-story/3bfaac36ec964211874c3bf8626cf0c5 (last accessed 2/8/18).

Financial Times Opinion (2018), 'China's belt and road initiative is falling short: The global infrastructure programme is struggling in key markets', *Financial Times*, 29 July 2018, available at www.ft.com/content/47d63fec-9185-11e8-b639-7680cedcc421 (last accessed 1/8/18).

Five Years of BRI (2018), 'Five years of the "one belt & one road" initiative and a new foreign relations to start a new silver road', *Guangming Daily*, 1 August, available at www.xinhuanet.com/fortune/2018-08/01/c_1123208611.htm (last accessed 2/8/18).

Fujiwara, Hidehito (2018), 'One belt, one road: A Japanese perspective', available at https://iias.asia/the-newsletter/article/one-belt-one-road-japanese-perspective (last accessed 30/7/18).

Gao, May Hongmei (2018), 'Globalization 5.0 Led by China: Powered by positives frames for BRI', in Zhang, Alon & Lattemann (2018).

Global Agenda Councils (2015), *Geo-economics: Seven Challenges to Globalization* (Geneva, Switzerland: World Economic Forum).

Golley, Jane & Ingle, Adam (2018), 'The belt and road initiative: How to win friends and influence people', in Jane Golley & Linda Jaivin (eds.), *China Story Yearbook 2017: Prosperity* (Canberra: The Australian National University Press).

Greer, Tanner (2018), 'One belt, one road, one big mistake', *Foreign Policy*, 6 December 2018, available at HTTPS://FOREIGNPOLICY.COM/2018/12/06/BRI-CHINA-BELT-ROAD-INITIATIVE-BLUNDER/ (last accessed 6/10/19).

Haass, Richard (2017), *A World in Disarray: American Foreign Policy and the Crisis of the Old Order* (Penguin: Penguin Press).

Hart, Melanie & Johnson, Blaine (2019), 'Mapping China's global governance ambitions', *Center for American Progress*, available at www.americanprogress.org/issues/security/reports/2019/02/28/466768/mapping-chinas-global-gover nance-ambitions/ (last accessed 18/10/19).

Hart-Landsberg, Martin (2018), 'A critical look at China's one belt, one road initiative', *Committee for the Abolition of Illegitimate Debt*, 10 October, available at www.cadtm.org/A-critical-look-at-China-s-One-Belt-One-Road-initiative (last accessed 6/10/19).

Hsu, Sara (2017), 'One belt trump's support for China's one belt, one road initiative is bad for US, Good for world', *Foreign Affairs*, 18 May 2017.

Hu, Anggang (2015), 'One belt one road: A geoeconomic revolution', A Speech delivered at An Economic Forum, Renming University, 3 June, available at http://mp.weixin.qq.com/s?__biz=MzA4MTQ0ODEwNg==&mid=206583737&idx=1&sn=890bbcb2e8360939f89cacfdbc6a5aed&scene=2&from=timeline&isappinstalled=0#rd (last accessed 3/6/15).

Huang, Ping (2019), 'To provide "a China plan" for the global governance of a human community of shared destiny', *Digest of Red Flag*, 24 October, available at www.qstheory.cn/dukan/hqwg/2019-10/24/c_1125147150.htm (last accessed 25/12/19).

ILO Covid-19, the ILO Covid 19 database, available at www.ilo.org/global/topics/coronavirus/impacts-and-responses/WCMS_824092/lang – en/index.htm (last accessed 5/5/22).

Jacques, Martin (2009), *When China Rules the World: The End of the Western World and the Birth of a New Global Order*, 2nd edition (New York/London: Penguin Books).

Japan Relocation (2020), 'Japan to pay firms to leave China, relocate production elsewhere as part of coronavirus stimulus', *Bloomberg*, 9 April, available at www.scmp.com/news/asia/east-asia/article/3079126/japan-pay-firms-leave-china-relocate-production-elsewhere-part (last accessed 8/5/22).

Jiang, Shengli (2018), 'Establishment of an international trade dispute settlement mechanism under the belt and road initiative', in Zhao (2018).

Kavalski, Eilian & Mayer, Maximilian (2019), 'China is now a power in Europe, but fears of interference in the EU are simplistic and misguided', *The Conversation*, 10 May, available at http://theconversation.com/china-is-now-a-power-in-europe-but-fears-of-interference-in-the-eu-are-simplistic-and-misguided-116193 (last accessed 15/10/19).

Klett, Tomas Casas I. & Oswald, Omar Ramon Serrano (2018), 'Free trade agreements as BRI's stepping-stone to multilateralism: Is the Sino-Swiss FTA the gold standard?' in Zhang, Alon & Lattemann (2018).

Kynge, James (2018), 'China's belt and road difficulties are proliferating across the world: Infrastructure project managers have been wrongfooted by local controversies', *Financial Times*, 9 July 2018, available at www.ft.com/content/fa3ca8ce-835c-11e8-a29d-73e3d454535d (last accessed 1/8/18).

Lee, Jaemin (2018), 'The belt and road initiative under existing trade agreements: Some food for thought on a new regional integration scheme', in Zhao (2018).

Leverett, Flynt & Wu, Bingbing (2016), 'The new silk road and China's evolving grand strategy', 77 *The China Journal* 110.

Li, Mingjiang (2020), 'The belt and road initiative: Geo-economics and Indo-Pacific security competition', 96 *International Affairs* 169.

Li, Xing (ed.) (2019), *Mapping China's 'One Belt One Road' Initiative* (Switzerland: Palgrave Macmillan).

Li, Xing (2019), 'China's pursuit of the "one belt one road" initiative: A new world order with Chinese characteristics?' in Li (2019).
Li, Zan (2016), 'To construct international law principles and path for the community of shared destiny', 6 *Research in International Law* (*Guoji Fa Yanjiu*) 48.
Lratz, Agatja, Feng, Allen & Wright, Logan (2019), 'New data on the "debt trap" question', *Rhodium Group*, 29 April 2019, available at https://rhg.com/research/new-data-on-the-debt-trap-question/ (last accessed 7/11/19).
Lu, Gang (2019), 'The BRI is facing three strategic constraints and its scope needs to be narrow down', *Xinhua*, 29 March 2019, available at http://tjapi.xinhuaapp.com/News/NewsDetail?id=412925&appId=317&projectId=51&from=timeline&isappinstalled=0 (last accessed 7/4/19).
Manuel, Ryan (2019), 'Twists in the belt and road', *China Leadership Monitor*, 1 September, available at www.prcleader.org/manuel-belt-road (last accessed 4/11/19).
Mazarr, Michael J., Heath, Timothy R. & Cevallos, Astrid Stuth (2018), *China and the International Order* (Santa Monica, CA:: The Rand Corporation), available at www.rand.org/pubs/research_reports/RR2423.html (last accessed 17/10/19).
McCawley, Peter (2019), 'Connecting the dots on the blue dot network', *The Interpreter*, 12 November, available at www.lowyinstitute.org/the-interpreter/connecting-dots-blue-dot-network (last accessed 2/5/22).
McCulloch, Daniel (2018), 'Australia, US and Japan sign regional pact', available at www.news.com.au/national/breaking-news/aust-us-japan-partners-for-indopacific/news-story/645aa8c37972d8f6f6a820d41ea6ba64 (last accessed 31/7/18).
McKinsey Global Institute (2018), 'How secure is the global financial system a decade after the crisis?' September 2018, available at www.mckinsey.com/industries/financial-services/our-insights/how-secure-is-the-global-financial-system-a-decade-after-the-crisis (last accessed 7/5/22).
Meltzer, Joshua P. (2017), 'China's one belt one road initiative: A view from the United States', *The ASAN Forum*, 19 June, available at www.brookings.edu/research/chinas-one-belt-one-road-initiative-a-view-from-the-united-states/ (last accessed 30/7/18).
Morris, David (2020), 'The three seas initiative: A European answer to China's belt and road?' *The Interpreter*, 26 October, available at www.lowyinstitute.org/the-interpreter/three-seas-initiative-european-answer-china-s-belt-and-road (last accessed 26/10/20).
Mulgan, Aurelia (2013), 'Japan, US and the TPP: The view from China', *East Asia Forum*, 5 May 2013, available at www.eastasiaforum.org/2013/05/05/japan-us-and-the-tpp-the-view-from-china/ (last accessed 17/10/13).
Needham, Kirsty (2018), 'China waives debt, promises "no imposition of will" on African nations', *The Sydney Morning Herald*, 4 September 2018, available at www.smh.com.au/world/asia/china-waives-debt-promises-no-imposition-of-will-on-african-nations-20180904-p501nr.html (last accessed 17/10/19).
Obama, Barack (2016), 'The TPP would let America, not China, lead the way on global trade', *Washington Post*, 2 May 2016, available at www.washingtonpost.com/opinions/president-obama-the-tpp-would-let-america-not-china-lead-the-way-on-global-trade/2016/05/02/680540e4–0fd0–11e6–93ae-50921721165d_story.html (last accessed 5/5/16)

Okano-Heijmans, Maaike & Kamo, Tomoki (2019), 'Engaging but not endorsing China's belt and road initiative', *Policy Brief*, available at www.clingendael.org/sites/default/files/2019-05/PB_China_Belt_and_Road_Initiative_May_2019.pdf (last accessed 15/10/19).

Oxford Covid-19, 'Oxford compendium of national legal responses to covid-19', available at https://oxcon.ouplaw.com/home/occ19 (last accessed 5/5/22).

Pathirana, Dilini (2018), 'Rising China and global investment governance: An overview of prospects and challenges', 4 *The Chinese Journal of Global Governance* 122.

People's Daily (2013), 'Who wants to re-shuffle the global trade cards', *People's Daily* (*Renmin Ribao*) (overseas edition), 18 April 2013, 6.

Perlez, Jane & Huang, Yufan (2017), 'Behind China's $1 trillion plan to shake up the economic order', *The New York Times*, 13 May 2017, available at www.nytimes.com/2017/05/13/business/china-railway-one-belt-one-road-1-trillion-plan.html (last accessed 9/8/18).

Prasad, Ravi (2018), 'EU ambassadors condemn China's belt and road initiative', *The Diplomat*, 21 April, available at https://thediplomat.com/2018/04/eu-ambassadors-condemn-chinas-belt-and-road-initiative/ (last accessed 22/7/18).

Rajah, Roland, Dayant, Alexandre & Pryke, Jonathan (2019), *Ocean of Debt? Belt and Road and Debt Diplomacy in the Pacific* (Lowy Institute), available at www.lowyinstitute.org/publications/ocean-debt-belt-and-road-and-debt-diplomacy-pacific (last accessed 28/10/19).

Ramirez, Steven (2006), 'Endogenous growth theory, status quo efficiency, and globalization', 17 (1) *Berkeley La Raza Law Journal* 1.

Ramskogler, Paul (2014), 'Tracing the origins of the financial crisis', (2) *OECD Journal: Financial Market Trends* 47.

Rapoz, Kenneth (2020), 'Overwhelming majority say time to "decouple" from China', *Forbes*, 27 April, available at www.forbes.com/sites/kenrapoza/2020/04/27/overwhelming-majority-say-time-to-decouple-from-china/#469bd39577a2 (last accessed 29/4/20).

Rogin, Josh (2018), 'The trump administration offers Asia an alternative to Chinese investment', *Washington Post*, 30 July, available at www.washingtonpost.com/news/josh-rogin/wp/2018/07/30/the-trump-administration-offers-asia-an-alternative-to-chinese-investment/?noredirect=on&utm_term=.c26d523fdde9&from=groupmessage&isappinstalled=0 (last accessed 1/8/18).

Roy, Anjian (2013), 'Bali is over, now look to the TPP summit in Singapore and beyond', 17 December, available at www.dnaindia.com/analysis/column-bali-is-over-now-look-to-the-tpp-summit-in-singapore-and-beyond-1936412 (last accessed 21/12/13).

Rudd, Kevin (2019), 'To decouple or not to decouple?' Speech for the Robert F. Ellsworth Memorial Lecture, 4 November, available at https://asiasociety.org/policy-institute/decouple-or-not-decouple (last accessed 10/11/21).

Russel, Daniel R. & Berger, Blake H. (2020), 'Weaponizing the belt and road initiative', A Report of the Asia Society Policy Institute, September, available at https://asiasociety.org/policy-institute/weaponizing-belt-and-road-initiative (last accessed 1/5/22)

Scholvin, Sören (2016), 'Geopolitics: An overview of concepts and empirical examples from international relations', FIIA Working Paper No 91, The Finish Institute of International Affairs, available at www.files.ethz.ch/isn/196701/wp91-Geopolitics.pdf (last accessed 8/8/18).

Scholvin, Sören & Wigell, Mikael (2018), 'Geo-economics as concept and practice in international relations: Surveying the state of the art', Working Paper No 102, Finish Institute of International Affairs, available at www.fiia.fi/en/publication/geo-economics-as-concept-and-practice-in-international-relations (last accessed 7/8/18).

Seshadri, V. S. (2013), 'Three deals that can change the world', available at www.thehindu.com/opinion/lead/three-deals-that-can-change-the-world/article5207438.ece (last accessed 21/12/13).

Shi, Jingxia (2018), 'The belt and road initiative and international law: An international public goods perspective', in Zhao (2018).

Skala-Kuhmann, Astrid (2019), 'European responses to BRI – An overdue assessment', (14) *Horizons*, available at www.cirsd.org/en/horizons/horizons-summer-2019-issue-no-14/european-responses-to-bri-an-overdue-assessment (last accessed 15/10/19).

Smith, Colby (2018), 'Belt and road, or debt trap?' *Financial Times*, 24 July 2018, available at https://ftalphaville.ft.com/2018/07/24/1532410200000/Belt-and-Road – or-debt-trap-/ (last accessed 1/8/18).

Song, Guoyou & Wen, Jin Yuan (2012), 'China's free trade agreement strategies', 35 (4) *Washington Quarterly* 107.

Stiglitz, Joseph E. (2016), 'The new geo-economics', *Project Syndicate*, 8 January, available at www.project-syndicate.org/commentary/hope-for-better-global-governance-by-joseph-e – stiglitz-2016–01?barrier=accesspaylog (last accessed 7/8/18).

Suokas, James (2018), 'China dismisses report on EU criticism against belt and road initiative', 19 April 2018, available at https://gbtimes.com/china-dismisses-report-on-eu-criticism-against-belt-and-road-initiative (last accessed 2/8/18).

Sussex, Matthew & Clarke, Michael (2017), 'One belt, one road, multiple rules-based orders', Policy Options Paper, No. 7, November 2017, National Security College, The Australian National University.

Symonds, Peter (2015), 'One belt, one road: China's response to the US "Pivot" ', 4 December, available at www.wsws.org/en/articles/2015/12/04/obor-d04.html (last accessed 30/7/18).

Tao, Jingzhou & Zhong, Mariana (2018), 'The changing rules of international dispute resolution in China's belt and road initiative', in Zhang, Alon & Lattemann (2018).

TPP India, 'Trans-pacific partnership: An Indian perspective', available at www.maritimeindia.org/srtc_report.html (last accessed 21/12/13).

Uren, David (2020), *Economic Coercion: Boycotts and Sanctions – Preferred Weapons of War* (The Australian Strategic Policy Institute), available at www.aspi.org.au/report/economic-coercion-boycotts-and-sanctions-preferred-weapons-war (last accessed 5/4/22).

Valero, Jorge (2019), 'European bloc not considering joining China's belt and road plans', *EURACTIV*, 27 April, available at www.euractiv.com/section/eu-china/news/european-bloc-not-considering-joining-chinas-belt-and-road-plans/ (last accessed 15/10/19).

van Leeuwen, Hans (2018), 'European Union shores up scrutiny of Chinese investments', *Financial Review*, 21 November, available at www.afr.com/news/policy/foreign-investment/european-union-shores-up-scrutiny-of-chinese-investments-20181121-h18559 (last accessed 18/2/19).

Varano, John (2021), 'Tearing up the belt and road initiative: Australia's rejection of China's new silk road in Victoria', *International Affairs*, 6 May, available at www.internationalaffairs.org.au/australianoutlook/tearing-up-the-belt-and-road-initiative-australias-rejection-of-chinas-new-silk-road-in-victoria/ (last accessed 1/5/22).

Viktor, Eszterhai (2017), 'The one belt one road from Germany's perspective', *Pallas Athene Geopolitical Research Institute*, 15 August, available at www.geopolitika.hu/en/2017/08/15/the-one-belt-one-road-from-germanys-perspective/ (last accessed 9/8/18).

Wade, Geoff (2018), 'China's "one belt, one road" initiative', Parliament of Australia, available at www.aph.gov.au/About_Parliament/Parliamentary_Departments/Parliamentary_Library/pubs/BriefingBook45p/ChinasRoad (last accessed 2/8/18).

Wang, Heng (2021), 'The belt and road initiative agreements: Characteristics, rationale, and challenges', 20 *World Trade Review* 282.

Wang, Honggang (2018), 'Emerging international order and China's role', in Deepak (2018).

Wang, Hongying & Rosenau, James N. (2009), 'China and global governance', 33 (3) *Asian Perspective* 5.

Wang, Jiangyu (2019), 'China's governance approach to the Belt and Road Initiative (BRI): Relations, partnership, and law', 14 (5) *Global Trade and Customs Journal* 222.

Wang, Zhiqiong June (2018), 'Beyond trade & investment: A contextual analysis of the misgivings over the "B&R" initiative', paper presented at the China-Oceania Legal Forum, organised by the China Law Society Guangzhou, 17–18 October 2018.

Wang, Zhiqiong June & Chen, Jianfu (2020), 'BRI 2.0: Cosmetic repair or change of course', 54 (5) *Journal of World Trade* 791.

White, Hugh (2013), *The China Choice: Why America Should Share Power*, 2nd edition (Melbourne: Black Inc).

White Paper (2019), 'China and the world in the new era', issued by the Information Office of the State Council, 27 September 2019. A Chinese text is available at www.gov.cn/zhengce/2019-09/27/content_5433889.htm (last accessed 15/10/19).

Wigell, Mikael & Vihma, Antto (2016), 'Geopolitics versus geoeconomics: The case of Russia's geostrategy and its effects on the EU', 3 *International Affairs* 605.

Wiśniewski, R. (2021), 'Economic sanctions as a tool of China's hybrid strategies', *Polish Political Science Yearbook*, available at https://heinonline.org/HOL/LandingPage?handle=hein.journals/ppsy50&div=42&id=&page= (last accessed 5/4/22).

Witt, Michael A. (2020), 'Prepare for the US and China to decouple', *Harvard Business Review*, 26 June 2020, available at https://hbr.org/2020/06/prepare-for-the-u-s-and-china-to-decouple (last accessed 28/6/20).

World Bank (2019), *Belt and Road Economics: Opportunities and Risks of Transport Corridors* (Washington, DC: World Bank).

World Bank Covid-19, 'The world bank covid-19 responses', available at www.worldbank.org/en/who-we-are/news/coronavirus-covid19.

Wray, L. Randall (2012), 'Global financial crisis: A minskyan interpretation of the causes, the fed's bailout, and the future', Working Paper No. 711, Levy Economics Institute of Bard College, available at www.levyinstitute.org/pubs/wp_711.pdf (last accessed 7/5/22).

Wroe, David (2018a), 'China makes inroads on Pacific aid but Australia remains the stalwart, study finds', *The Age*, 8 August, available at www.theage.com.au/politics/federal/china-makes-inroads-on-pacific-aid-but-australia-remains-the-stalwart-study-finds-20180808-p4zw8b.html (last accessed 9/8/18).

Wroe, David (2018b), 'Foreign affairs ministry opts for secrecy over China infrastructure agreement', *The Age*, 30 July, available at www.theage.com.au/politics/federal/foreign-affairs-ministry-opts-for-secrecy-over-china-infrastructure-agreement-20180730-p4zufm.html (last accessed 31/7/18).

WTO Covid-19, available at www.wto.org/english/tratop_e/covid19_e/covid19_e.htm (last accessed 8/5/22).

WTO Covid-19 Trade, 'COVID-19: Measures affecting trade in goods', available at www.wto.org/english/tratop_e/covid19_e/trade_related_goods_measure_e.htm (last accessed 8/5/22).

Xi, Jinping (2019a), 'Speech delivered at the press conference during the second belt and road forum for international cooperation', *Beijing*, 27 April, available at www.yidaiyilu.gov.cn/xjbyydyl/xjbls/90618.htm (last accessed 27/10/19).

Xi, Jinping (2019b), 'Working together to deliver a brighter future for the belt and road cooperation', A keynote speech delivered at the Belt and Road Forum for International Cooperation 2019, Beijing, 26 April 2019, available at www.yidaiyilu.gov.cn/xjbyydyl/xjbls/90618.htm (last accessed 27/10/19).

Xinhua (2015a), 'The visit to the UK by president Xi Jinping reflects changes in international order', *Xinhua*, 26 October 2015, available at http://news.xinhuanet.com/politics/2015-10/26/c_128359512.htm (last accessed 26/10/15).

Xinhua (2015b), 'The beginning in establishing a new international economic order', *Xinhua*, 26 October 2015, available at http://news.xinhuanet.com/world/2015-10/26/c_1116939216.htm (last accessed 26/10/15).

Xiong, Ping & Tomasic, Roman (2019), 'Soft law, state-owned enterprises and dispute resolution on PRC's belt and road – towards an emerging legal order?' 49 (3) *Hong Kong Law Journal* 1025.

Yuan, Feng (2019), 'The one belt one road initiative and China's multilayered multilateralism', in Li (2019).

Zhang, Ketian (2018), 'Calculating bully – explaining Chinese coercion', PhD thesis, MIT, 2018, available at https://dspace.mit.edu/handle/1721.1/122472 (last accessed 5/4/22).

Zhang, Wenxian, Alon, Ilan & Lattemann, Christoph (eds.) (2018), *China's Belt and Road Initiative: Changing the Rules of Globalization* (London: Palgrave Macmillan).

Zhao, Hong (2016), 'China's one belt one road: An overview of the debate', Yusof Ishak Institute, Singapore, available at https://pdfs.semanticscholar.org/81e7/5b1d8083ac26b9ed66c36f3c59f49beb7192.pdf?_ga=2.129604613.861081360.1576283711-1713749923.1576283711 (last accessed 14/12/19).

Zhao, Yun (2018), *International Governance and the Rule of Law in China under the Belt and Road Initiative* (New York: Cambridge University Press).

5 Against the Law of the Jungle

The Need for Efficient, Effective and Impartial Dispute Resolution

1. Introduction

Chapter 1 established that the liberal economic order is the foundation of the present multilateral trade regulatory regime. Chapters 2—4 examined the various challenges that have been mounted to that foundation and suggest that the multilateral trade regime is in fact a dynamic system that has so far sustained, to a varying degree, the various challenges made at different times. These challenges have, however, made the multilateral system much more complicated over time and, hence, much more prone to trade disputes. The future of the multilateral trade regime depends, to a very significant extent, but not entirely, on how its dispute resolution mechanism might respond to and resolve the disputes among the WTO members.

The WTO dispute resolution mechanism is described as a 'precious system' and, because of its much-improved rules and processes made at the Uruguay Round, 'the jewel in the crown of multilateralism' (Moore, 2003: 109). Unfortunately, this crown jewel is, at the moment, having its own share of problems, as the dispute resolution mechanism seems unable to resolve the disputes about its reforms that are needed to improve its efficiency, effectiveness and, most of all, impartiality and fairness. The reviews in Chapters 2—4 reveal that the whole multilateral system is having some problems and need reform, but none is more important and urgent than that for the dispute resolution mechanism itself.

This chapter first reviews, very briefly, the dispute resolution mechanism under the GATT. It then moves to analyse the same under the WTO, focusing on the improvement made at the Uruguay Round of negotiations. In Section 4, the current problems to the dispute resolution mechanisms under the WTO and the proposed reforms are closely examined. This chapter then proceeds to analyse issues that are not covered by the WTO dispute resolution mechanisms but often cause major trade disruption in our contemporary

DOI: 10.4324/9781003275510-6

world. This chapter will conclude that a resolution to the current impasse in WTO reforms as well as disputes outside the WTO mechanisms is critical, if the multilateral trade regime is to survive the various challenges it now faces.

2. From Power-Based Mechanisms to Adjudication among Equals

Strictly speaking, GATT does not have a dispute resolution mechanism; it does not contain specific provisions that define disputes nor any provisions that establish a dispute settlement procedure. What were, after the establishment and operation of GATT, later referred to as the unintended yet *de facto* GATT dispute resolution mechanisms (Lester, Mercurio, & Davies, 2018: 151) were consultation and negotiation procedures established by Arts XXII & XXIII of the GATT and, more importantly, jurisprudence established thereunder through the years before the WTO was established in 1995. Thus, Arts XXII & XXIII of GATT were seen as the core of the GATT dispute settlement procedures (Islam, 1993: 232). The lack of provisions for dispute resolution in the original GATT is generally attributed to the fact that GATT was originally meant to be an agreement to be administered by an 'international trade organisation' (Lester, Mercurio, & Davies, 2018: 150), which, as discussed in Chapter 1, did not come into existence until the establishment of the WTO in 1995.

Art XXII, entitled 'Consultation', requires parties to afford 'adequate opportunity for consultation' with respect to any matter affecting the operation of the GATT, not only bilaterally but also multilaterally among contracting parties. Art XXIII, slightly longer in length in the original form but significantly supplemented and clarified by four additional 'Decisions'/'Understanding' adopted respectively in 1966, 1979, 1982 and 1989 (for specific decisions, see Lester, Mercurio, & Davies, 2018: footnote 2, at 152), is entitled 'Nullification or Impairment'. Basically, a GATT member may make a representation to another party if the first party considers that its membership benefits are being nullified or impaired or that the attainment of GATT objectives is being frustrated by the other party because of the following:

(1) the failure of another contracting party to carry out its obligations under the GATT, or
(2) the application by another contracting party of any measure, whether or not it conflicts with the provisions of the GATT, or
(3) the existence of any other situation.

The idea of making such a representation is to have the 'grievances' addressed by the other party making 'satisfactory adjustment of the matter' within a reasonable time. This then is often conducted through bilateral or multilateral negotiations and consultation. Procedures after the failure of negotiations and consultation were essentially developed after the conclusion of the GATT and, as such, they are significantly supplementary to the provisions of Art XXIII.

In a nutshell, in a GATT dispute, upon the failure of negotiations or consultations, the aggrieved party may refer the dispute to the GATT Council with a request for the establishment of a panel of experts or, for less complicated cases, for the appointment of a working party. This 'third-party' panel dispute resolution emerged in 1949 and eventually became a standard means in 1952 (Trebilcock, Howse, & Eliason, 2012: 173). The Panel or working party's report on the dispute then makes 'appropriate recommendations' for its resolution. These recommendations were then subject to adoption by the GATT Council on a consensus basis. Although the processes became more legalistic in nature from the 1950s onwards, the GATT processes nevertheless suffered from some 'conspicuous shortcoming' (Lester, Mercurio, & Davies, 2018: 151–152) – the so called 'double veto' embedded in the 'dispute resolution' system that had an emphasis on negotiation and conciliation.

The 'double veto' was of course 'achieved' through the consensus requirements imbedded in the original drafting of the GATT. The previously mentioned Panel, upon the completion of its 'investigation', is to prepare and submit a report to the GATT Council. However, the report is to be accepted by consensus before it may have any legally binding effect. The so-called acceptance by consensus simply means that the party being complained of has a right of veto. Further, assuming the report is not vetoed, the report can still be ignored by the 'offending' party and, only at this point, may the GATT Council authorise penalties. Against all common sense, such penalties could only be adopted by consensus of the Council. In other words, any penalty can, once again, be vetoed by the party against which the penalty is to be imposed.

With the embedment of the double veto power, the GATT dispute settlement process was essentially a diplomacy-based conciliatory process, with its effectiveness being heavily dependent on moral and political pressures rather than legal force (for further discussions on GATT dispute resolution, see Jackson, 1989: ch.4; Lester, Mercurio, & Davies, 2018: 149–153). In fact, the fundamental nature of the GATT dispute settlement is unique in that:

> . . . the central concept of the GATT dispute settlement mechanism is not primarily violation of the General Agreement, or of obligations

> assumed thereunder. It is curtailment, in the broadest sense of the word, of the benefits flowing from the Agreement, or of the objectives pursued by the entire Agreement or by individual provisions of it.
>
> (Pescatore & Lowenfelf, 1992: 4)

The GATT dispute settlement process, despite its inbuilt weaknesses, was a reasonably successful mechanism: of the 355 cases brought to the GATT, concessions were obtained by the 'plaintiffs' in 64% cases. Among these, concessions were more likely to be offered before a panel ruling was made, suggesting negotiation and conciliation were the principal methods of dispute settlement rather than legal compliance with panel 'rulings'.[1]

However, and despite its relative success in negotiating and conciliating disputes, the GATT dispute resolution mechanism was not only weak; it had also been criticised for long delays, inconsistencies, uncertainties, inadequacy of compliance and enforcement, among other deficiencies (Kohona, 1994: 24). Although one could argue that negotiation and conciliation are the principal means employed in all international dispute resolution,[2] trade disputes are not meant to be political in nature[3] and, as such, some form of adjudication is required to ensure consistency, effectiveness and compliance. Further, the Uruguay Round negotiations were meant to establish a *de jure* organisation that would also expand trade regulation well beyond the traditional subject-matters of trade in goods. It is therefore not surprising that dispute resolution was one of the major issues for the Uruguay Round negotiations and the new mechanism established thereunder now forms a key feature of the WTO and represents a most significant achievement in the Uruguay Round of negotiations.

The central piece of the WTO dispute resolution mechanism is the Understanding on Rules and Procedures Governing the Settlement of Disputes (hereinafter the Understanding), being Annex 2 of the WTO Agreement. The Understanding's fundamental change as a result of the Uruguay Round is a movement from compromise-intended conciliation in the GATT to rule-based adjudication in the WTO. Although the legal instrument is entitled 'Understanding', a term that sounds like a less formal treaty, it is defined

1 For detailed statistical analysis, see Busch & Reinhard, 2003. See also Trebilcock, Howse, & Eliason, 2012: 177, which suggests a higher success rate during the period from 1948 to 1989.

2 Indeed, GATT dispute resolution was a most successful international dispute resolution mechanism at the time when major reforms were to be adopted at the Uruguay Round. See Lester, Mercurio, & Davies, 2018: 153.

3 As will be discussed later, trade disputes are increasingly caused by political disagreements in our increasingly geopolitically contested world.

as an integral part of the WTO (Art II:2 of the WTO Agreement). In other words, this 'Understanding' is a full treaty that is legally binding.

Also importantly, just like GATT having been transformed from a treaty into an organisation, WTO dispute resolution mechanism is now firmly entrenched in an institutional setting, governing not only GATT disputes but also disputes arising out of the so-called 'Covered Agreements'.[4] Put simply, the WTO dispute resolution mechanism has a comprehensive, though not a completely centralised,[5] 'jurisdiction' over disputes in relation to agreements under the WTO, including GATT 1994, GATS, TRIPs, as well as the plurilateral trade agreements.[6]

Institutionally, a Dispute Settlement Body (DSB, which is in fact the same as the General Council of the WTO) is set up[7] and, more importantly, a standing Appellate Body (AB) is established to review the legal basis for decisions in the WTO dispute resolution mechanism. While the practice of establishing panels continues, the process of adopting a panel report (or a report of the Appellate Body) will be automatic (unless there is a consensus not to adopt the report – the so-called 'negative consensus') and, thus, the double veto power in the GATT dispute settlement system is eliminated.

On paper at least, strict deadlines are laid down by the Understanding for each stage of the dispute resolution process (including time limit for consultation) as well as the implementation of the panel's final recommendations once they are accepted by the DSB. Clearly, such deadlines are established to address the problem of GATT members using the various processes (including consultation) as a delay tactic. Unilateral action, before a panel has reached its decision, is prohibited and any action that is taken after a panel has come to a decision must first be approved by the DSB. This prohibition of unilateral actions is to ensure that WTO dispute settlement processes are based on an adjudication process rather than the previous power-based negotiations.

4 Those are contained in Art 1:1 and Appendix I of the Understanding.

5 Some of the WTO agreements, understandings and other legal instruments do contain their own dispute resolution provisions and these provisions are deemed special or additional rules and procedures that their application prevails over the provisions in the Understanding.

6 The applicability of the Understanding to the Plurilateral Trade Agreements is a slightly more complicated matter: essentially, a decision needs to be adopted by the parties to each agreement setting out the terms of the application of the Understanding to the individual agreement, including any special or additional rules or procedures for inclusion in Appendix 2, as notified to the DSB (see Item C of Appendix I to the Understanding).

7 This DSB will be the General Council of the WTO during the interval of the Ministerial Conference and working under the name of DSB: Art IV:3 of the WTO Agreement.

In short, institutionally and procedurally, the dispute settlement mechanism under the WTO is designed to adjudicate disputes on the basis of legal rights under, or alleged violations of, WTO agreements. However, the processes of negotiation, conciliation, and the use of good offices are still part of the dispute settlement processes.[8] Further, detailed and transparent panel working procedures, which are also flexibly supplemented for each penal established (Arts 12–15, 18, and 20) are published to ensure transparency, neutrality and impartiality of the processes. Not surprisingly, the establishment of the dispute settlement mechanism is regarded as one of the most significant achievements at the Uruguay Round of negotiations and the dispute settlement system is lauded as the 'crown jewel' of the WTO. Indeed, until the recent setback (the total paralysis of the Appellate Body (AB) since December 2019, discussed later), the WTO dispute settlement mechanism worked as one of the most outstanding dispute settlement mechanisms in international law: between 1995 and the end of 2020, some 445 panel reports, Appellate Body reports and arbitral awards or decisions were made to settle some 548 disputes referred to the DSB by WTO members.[9] Reflecting the changing balance of powers in international trade, there has also been a shift from Trans-Atlantic disputes to Trans-Pacific ones (notably, the raising number of cases involving China) (VanGrasstek, 2013: 248–249).

3. From the Crown Jewel to a Crown of Thorns[10]

The WTO dispute settlement mechanism is, however, far from perfect. In fact, it did not take much time before various problems began to emerge.

One of the important features of WTO mechanism are the various deadlines set for the different stages of the dispute settlement processes. However, these deadlines were often not met in practice. Further, the various processes, especially the appeal process, were used by some countries as a delay tactic to obtain enough time to implement their non-conforming policies and practices. The formalistic approach to adjudication also entails high costs, the need for specialist expertise, and the constraint on consideration outside strict trade disputes, such as environment protection in international trade (Harris, 2004: 307–332). High costs and the need for specialist expertise also posed difficulties for many developing but especially least

8 In fact, Members may also opt for arbitration under Art 25 of the Understanding. Also, certain concessions are allowed for developing but especially the least developed countries. See Art 24 of the Understanding.

9 See WTO, www.wto.org/english/tratop_e/dispu_e/dispustats_e.htm (9/11/21).

10 Creamer, 2019.

developed countries to access the mechanism, not to mention making full use of the mechanism. And finally, when the disputes are between a large and a small country, any 'authorised' retaliation measures for the small country makes little sense against the large country. These and many other technical problems inevitably undermine the efficiency and effectiveness of trade dispute settlement at the WTO.[11]

As already mentioned previously, this imperfect system continued to work reasonably well, at least in terms of dispute cases settled, until the total paralysis of the Appellate Body (AB) in December 2019 when the AB had only one member and was unable to establish any legally required review panel.[12]

The AB is a unique and innovative feature adopted by the Understanding, which gives the clearest signal that the WTO dispute resolution process is of an adjudicative nature. The AB is composed of seven members, each serving on the basis of a four-year term which can be renewed once. Members of the AB are legally required to be 'persons of recognised authority, with demonstrated expertise in law, international trade and the subject matter of the covered agreements generally' (Art 17 (3) of the Understanding). However, unlike the adoption of panel or AB reports, the decision to appoint an AB member is by consensus of the Dispute Settlement Body (which is the General Council working in a different capacity) (Art 2.4 of the Understanding). Thus, such an appointment can be blocked, theoretically, by any member of the WTO.

A panel to deal with an appeal requires three members, and a panel decision is required to be made within 90 days of the appeal being lodged. The rulings made by the panels will be reviewed by the remaining members of the Appellate Body to ensure consistency of decision making (VanGrasstek, 2013: 240, referring to the author's interview with Mr. Bhatia on 27 September 2012). Like the WTO dispute resolution mechanism as a whole, the AB had worked reasonably well, though not without some technical and practical problems such as delays in decision-making, and its rulings are generally well regarded in practice as providing a consistent body of law (VanGrasstek, 2013: 241).

On the surface, the crisis of December 2019 was caused by the US block of appointments of new members to the AB to replace those whose

11 For detailed analysis of the WTO dispute resolution and problems identified therein, see Trebilcock, Howse, & Eliason, 2012: Ch 5; Lester, Mercurio, & Davies, 2018: Ch 5; Matsushita, Schoenbaum, Mavroidis, & Hahn, 2015: Ch 4. For a short summary, see Baweja, 2020.

12 The term of the last member, Professor Dr. Hong Zhao from China, expired on 30 November 2020. See www.wto.org/english/tratop_e/dispu_e/appellate_body_e.htm (9/5/22).

terms expired at different times since 2017 (Payosova, Hufbauer, & Schott, 2018).[13] In reality, however, the causes for the crisis are various and they are deeply rooted in the original design of the AB as well as its practical development.[14] Fundamentally, the WTO is meant to be a developing system but the stall of the Doha Round of the negotiations meant that it became stationary and stagnant, leaving many 'grey' areas without clarity and many newly emerged trade issues and disputes without legal rules to go by.[15] Under these circumstances, the developing countries, reflecting their urgent need to address specific incidents in individual occasions, focused on the obvious measures like antidumping and countervailing duties. The developed countries, taking the opportunity to request the panel or AB to define the scope of the various ambiguous concepts, and clarify the grey areas, are more concerned with the bigger picture of their trade agreement obligations and focused more on the less observable trade measures like the subsidies, other domestic measures, export restrictions and so on (see Bown, 2009). Further, different from the GATT period, WTO agreements are now subject to 'judicial' interpretation, and it is in this context, the WTO dispute settlement panels, but especially the AB, are being criticised for being open to 'non-trade' issues and hence 'inventing the law' (Trebilcock, Howse, & Eliason, 2012: 215–216, which provides further analysis on this issue and other problems in relation to the Appellate Body), or 'legislate through dispute settlement' (Stewart, 2018). Obviously, the underlying cause is the lack of 'legislative' development that caused 'judicial' activism to develop in the absence of clear legal rules.[16] These occurred at the same time when the significance of the WTO framework was undermined by the emergence of the negotiations of large regional trade agreements, such as the TPP and

13 The Trump Administration is often blamed for the AB crisis, and its Administration was accused of waging a 'stealth war' and 'killing the WTO from the inside'. See Creamer,2019: 51. In reality, the Obama Administration first blocked the reappointment of an AB member in 2011 and another member's reappointment in 2016. See Rathore & Bajpai, 2020.

14 For comprehensive reviews and analyses of the various issues in this regard, see Hart & Murrill, 2021; Lehne, 2019.

15 See Creamer, 2019. This is, of course, not to say that other problems are not important. For instance, the increasingly complicated processes, leading not only to delays (some cases took 16 years to settle), expenses and complex decisions (some decisions amounted to 1,000 pages in length), have the potential to exclude many members from access to WTO dispute settlement. See Tai, 2021.

16 One may argue, of course, that the reform of the Understanding is not part of the single undertaking of the Doha negotiations and its reform could move forward separately. In reality, it is linked with the Doha negotiations. See Trebilcock, Howse, & Eliason, 2012: 216.

the RCEP, which in turn further undermine the urgently needed reforms of the WTO.

As already mentioned previously, the AB has no members at the moment and has thus ceased to function, yet, panel reports are continuing to be appealed by losing parties 'into the void', leaving disputes unresolved (Lester, 2022).[17] This is so, not because there are no proposals to address the current impasse at the WTO dispute settlement mechanism,[18] but because none of the proposals is yet to obtain the consensus of all members, and most of them focus on resolving technical problems. In fact, there is currently an interim mechanism, the 'Multi-party interim appeal arbitration arrangement' established, in April 2020, on the basis of Art 25 of the Understanding,[19] by 19 members of the WTO.[20] However useful it might be as an interim mechanism, it does not resolve the problems that led to the current crisis with the AB (see Gao, 2021).

4. Law of the Jungle and the Power of the Powerful

The dispute settlement mechanism is not only a jewel of the WTO; it is also an ambitious arrangement. Although a WTO member is almost always a member of some other bilateral or regional agreements, Art 23 of the DSU basically requires that trade disputes be brought to and redress sought from the WTO mechanism, the so-called exclusivity of WTO procedures.[21] On the other hand, however, for a 'judicial' process to be initiated, that is, to request the establishment of a panel, the complainant must first 'identify the specific measures at issue and provide a brief summary of the legal basis of the complaint sufficient to present the problem clearly' (Art 6.2 of the Understanding). Further, following the general 'judicial' approach, the complainant must assume the burden of proof (Trebilcock, Howse, & Eliason, 2012: 192–195). These provisions assume that there are some degrees of certainty and transparency in trade disputes and that members are always

17 As of April 2022, there were 24 decisions by dispute settlement panels that have not been finalised and were in limbo (see Ellard, 2022), and the number could only increase.

18 For a summary of some of the proposals, see Payosova, Hufbauer, & Schott, 2018. For some official proposals, see Communication, 2018a; Communication, 2018b; WTO, 2018. For further discussion, see Charnovitz, 2017; Bahri, 2019.

19 https://trade.ec.europa.eu/doclib/press/index.cfm?id=2143

20 These are Australia, Brazil, Canada, China, Chile, Colombia, Costa Rica, the European Union, Guatemala, Hong Kong, China, Iceland, Mexico, New Zealand, Norway, Pakistan, Singapore, Switzerland, Ukraine and Uruguay. It should be pointed out that this mechanism is also open to other members to join if they wish.

21 This is so with some limited exceptions. See Trebilcock, Howse, & Eliason, 2012: 213.

bona fide in complying with the WTO rules. The reality is very different, and the actual practice is far from this assumption/presumption.

Critically, as in any international relations, there are always formidable difficulties in attempting to subject the powerful countries to international rules, even though international law is precisely meant to address the problem. In this context and during the pre-WTO era, careful studies had earlier demonstrated that the US had a disproportionate level of non-compliance of GATT rulings (Trebilcock, Howse,·& Eliason, 2012: 177). Further, it is no secret that the US Trade Representative (USTR) frequently determined, unilaterally, violations of US rights by foreign governments and imposed retaliation measures without the involvement of GATT. It was only in 1998 when the EU brought a claim against the US challenging this US practice, the panel report eventually held that the US government authorities were not in a position to determine whether there were breaches of WTO obligations by other members and banned unilateral enforcement.[22] It is also no secret that the US's acceptance to the WTO's dispute settlement mechanism is simply a compromise in exchange for the acceptance of broad substantive obligations in the Uruguay Round, and it did not change the US's assumption of continuing its implementation of a unilateral trade mechanism even after the conclusion of the WTO Agreements, and this was particularly the situation in the 2010s during the Trump administration. Indeed, under the 'American Exceptionalism' ideology (Deudney & Meiser, 2012: 21), the US trade policies and measures were never hesitant to shy away from protecting their own interests over complying with international instruments and obligations. This 'American Exceptionalism' went even further under the slogan 'America First' put forward by Donald Trump in 2016 (Sanger & Haberman, 2016). Not surprisingly, the US government under the Trump Administration frequently disputed with other major economies and applied trade measures against them, including China, the EU, Japan and so on. More broadly, there has been a general trend against globalisation in favour of local protectionism. There has long been a struggle in trade policy between the liberalisation and protectionism around the world, but in recent years, the trend towards protectionism took over, as demonstrated by the Brexit, the trade war between the US and China, as well as the crisis of the WTO (see Sheldon et al., 2018; Petersmann, 2018). Nevertheless, 'American Exceptionalism' or 'America First' is, more or less, transparent and, most importantly, could only be implemented through law or transparent policies or legal measures imposed by the government. This means that

22 United States – Sections 301–310 of the Trade Act 1974, WT/DS152/R, 22 December 1999.

they could be challenged at the WTO or, in some cases, at regional forums and, indeed, they have been so challenged.

China's rise presents a rather different set of problems. As already discussed in the previous chapters, China does not only benefit from its economic liberalisation – a promise for its WTO membership – but also becomes a major force influencing the global trade policy. China became the second largest economy in 2010 from the sixth largest in 2001 when it joined the WTO.[23] China's GDP had grown from US$1.3 trillion in 2001 to US$14.3 trillion in 2019, or 12.3% of the US's GDP in 2001 to 66.8% in 2019.[24] The rapid growth of China's economy broke the power balance of the WTO Members when WTO Agreements were negotiated or even when China joined the WTO. The US and other developed countries complained that China abused the WTO system and benefited unfairly from its participation. The fractious relationship with China was evidenced by the controversy in relation to its non-market economy status and China's status as a developing country (Wu, 2016: 300–316). These issues are reflected in the US's Trade Policy focusing on the WTO reforms in relation to the self-declaration of development status and non-market economy issues (The USTR, 2019).

Misusing or abusing of WTO rules is one thing, however, China using its newly acquired economic powers in an extra-legal manner is another thing. Here, the current strained trade relationship between China and Australia offers an excellent example of impotence of the WTO dispute settlement mechanism – a crown jewel that contains a fatal weakness.

Australia was one of the first Western countries to establish diplomatic relations with China, with Australia's recognition of the People's Republic of China (PRC) in 1972. A bilateral relationship between the two countries developed reasonably smoothly and, in 2014, the bilateral relationship was defined as a 'comprehensive strategic partnership', with the China – Australia Free Trade Agreement (ChAFTA) entering into force in December 2015. By then, China had been Australia's largest trading partner in goods and services for several years, accounting for nearly one third of Australia's global trade in 2019 (Department of Foreign Affairs and Trade (DFAT), undated). However, the China-Australia relationship was to deteriorate soon after its peak in 2014.

23 Statistics from the United Nations: https://unstats.un.org/unsd/snaama/Index; International Monetary Fund: www.imf.org/external/pubs/ft/weo/2010/02/weodata/download.aspx and the World Bank: https://databank.worldbank.org/home.aspx.

24 Statistics from the World Bank: https://data.worldbank.org/country

The first cracks in the relationship occurred in 2012 when the Australian intelligence agency detected a sophisticated intrusion into Australia's telecommunications systems by Huawei (Robertson & Tarabay, 2021).[25] This intrusion eventually led to Australia's decision to ban the participation of Huawei in Australia's 5G construction in 2018 (Hartcher, 2021). 2018 also saw the introduction of a comprehensive package of legislative reforms by Australia in relation to foreign interference.[26] In 2020, in response to the Covid-19 pandemic came Australia's call for an international inquiry into the origin of the virus (Timeline, 2020). As a consequence, the relationship between the two countries began to deteriorate rapidly.

China did not hide its anger with Australia and, through the government-controlled media, began to disseminate a message that China will exercise its economic muscle and punish Australia (Hanson, Currey, & Beattie, 2020). Soon, reports began to emerge that various trade 'sanctions' were being imposed on Australia.[27] There were then reports of the 'go-slow' practice at Chinese customs to hold up the clearance of Australia wines. This was followed by new administrative hurdles imposed by China on the importation of Australian beef, lobsters, fruits, cotton, timber and the massive delay or plain refusal to allow Australia shipments of coal entering Chinese ports (and hence stranded outside of ports) (Hanson, Currey, & Beattie, 2020: 29–30; Timeline, 2020; Ryan, 2020; Tan, 2020; Choudhury, 2020). Warnings were also issued by China on the so-call 'racist attacks' on Chinese students and tourists in Australia (Hanson, Currey, & Beattie, 2020: 29–30; Timeline, 2020; Ryan, 2020; Tan, 2020; Choudhury, 2020). Importantly, most of these 'bans' or 'sanctions' were imposed by China without any formal notice being issued; they were carried out by oral orders passed through various agents, brokers, industrial and commerce chambers and so on, thus officially there were no 'bans' or 'sanctions' (Tan, 2020). China's actions on restricting/hindering Australia's trade were, put simply, extra-legal measures for which there are little legal channels to challenge their legality nor, indeed methods to gather evidence as required by the WTO.

25 Later reports suggest that Huawei was involved in a number of other espionage events. See Dube, 2022.

26 Principally, this includes the National Security Legislation Amendment (Espionage and Foreign Interference) Act 2018; and The Foreign Influence Transparency Scheme Act 2018.

27 In fact, China-Australia relationship became sore in 2016 when Australia criticised China's land reclamation in the South China Sea and China then blocked Australia's shipment of pasteurised milk. See Hanson, Currey, & Beattie, 2020: 31. 2018 however saw the rapid deterioration of the bilateral relationship.

Some legal measures were later imposed by China, such as anti-dumping and anti-subsidy duties on Australian barley in May 2020 and on Australian wines a few months later. However, informal trade bans remain the principal method used by China[28] to disrupt the Australia/China trading relationship. Such practices are not only opaque; they are extra-legal, outside of coverage of the WTO or any other bilateral and regional agreements. This conduct by China is only possible in a centrally controlled non-market economy and easily done in a country where the Communist Party has openly asserted its leadership in all political, economic and social life and in all processes (Chen, 2016, 2020). Further, it must be remembered that, because of the long process entailed in resolving anti-dumping or anti-subsidy cases, formal legal measures and the consequential dispute settlement process at the WTO are not unfrequently used as a delay tactic that often achieves the objective of destroying market access of the supposedly 'offending' party.

The only avenue to address such informal sanctions is consultation, a traditional and long-held practice in Chinese dispute resolution (see Wang & Chen, 2019). However, China simply closed the door to such consultation, despite the existence of a bilateral trade and investment treaty which provides methods for dispute resolution including consultation.[29] In fact, China had blocked all China-Australian ministerial meetings since November 2019,[30] and in early May 2021, China 'indefinitely' suspended the China-Australia Strategic Economic Dialogue, thus ending another forum where economic disputes might otherwise be discussed (Crossley & Needham, 2021). There is no sign, at the time of writing, that such blocks and bans would be lifted by China any time soon.[31] Indeed, China has now made it clear to Australia that such high-level dialogue would only resume if Australia meets

28 For instance, China has blocked Australia's coal export, which was the third-largest export to China, since 2018, but there has, until this day, no formal ban issued at all.

29 That is, the China – Australia Free Trade Agreement (ChAFTA) which entered into force in December 2015.

30 According to Country Brief, Foreign Affairs and Trade, Australian Government, the last meeting between China and Australia occurred at a ministerial meeting in November 2019. DFAT, undated. The first meeting, since then, at ministerial level between China and Australia only occurred in mid-June 2022, when the two defence ministers met on the sidelines of the Shangri-La Dialogue defence summit in Singapore.

31 It is simply too early to say that the defence ministers' meeting in June 2022 and subsequent meeting of foreign ministers as signifying in any way the end of China's ban on government contact. It should also be pointed out that Australia is not the only country that has been subject to such 'sanctions' by China; some 27 countries in Europe, North America, East Asia and Oceania have suffered the same fate when these countries disagreed with China in their various international relationships. See Hanson, Currey, & Beattie, 2020: 11.

certain conditions such as the so-called '14 grievances' (Payne, 2021).[32] In response, Australia has made clear that it would not meet such a condition, or in the words of the then Prime Minister of Australia, Scott Morrison, 'no country would do that' (Payne, 2021).

In the absence of any government-to-government consultation and formal government measures imposing sanctions, the WTO dispute resolution mechanism is impotent. This is because the injured party simply does not have a cause of action nor indeed any formal evidence to support complaint or its legal action (if any taken).[33] Under these circumstances, purely legal and technical analyses of WTO dispute cases do not capture all the complexities of international trade relations and the realities of that trade, and potentially mislead in their conclusions (see e.g., Zhou & Laurenceson, 2022).

This so-call China-Australia trade dispute is described by some as 'the most salient present instance of trade coverage being weaponised for political ends' (Financial Times, 2022). Trade here is blatantly used as a means of economic coercion and, as such, the dispute is not about trade at all (Hanson, Currey, & Beattie, 2020; Zhang, 2018; Wiśniewski, 2021; Blumenthal, 2018; Chen, 2019; Uren, 2020). One may argue that trade sanctions are frequently used by powerful countries, notably the US. In the case of US, as just mentioned previously, one can at least say that sanctions are imposed through a legal process in accordance with its relevant domestic laws and such sanctions are implemented in a reasonably transparent manner.[34] In the case of China-Australia trade, most 'sanctions' were never announced and mostly implemented informally. And, even if China's conduct is a 'sanction' against Australia,[35] it is not even clear what that 'sanction' is against or

32 In November 2020, the Chinese embassy in Canberra deliberately leaked a dossier of 14 disputes to several Australian media outlets, and this document has now become the 'infamous list of 14 grievances'. See Kearsley, Bagshaw, & Galloway, 2020, which includes a full text of the '14 grievances'. These '14 grievances' include decisions by the Australian Foreign Investment Review Board, Australian legislation on foreign interference, Australian criticisms on Chinese policies in Xinjiang and Hong Kong, Australia's ban on Huawei, and Australia's call for an international inquiry into the origin of COVID-19.

33 See Art 6.2 of the Understanding and the Working Procedures thereunder.

34 On US use of economic sanctions, see Haass, 1998; Hanania, 2020. For a summary discussion, see Coates, 2019.

35 It should be noted that China only issued a very brief Anti-Foreign Sanctions Law in June 2021. This Law authorises the Chinese government to impose sanctions against foreign persons or organisations if the country of the foreign persons or organisations imposes sanctions or discrimination against China or interferes with China's domestic affairs. Prior to this Law, The Ministry of Commerce issued the Provisions of the Unreliable Entity List in September 2020 and the Rules on Blocking Unjustified Extra-territorial Application of

about other than that China does not like certain policies of Australia. These Australian policies are openly and transparently implemented by a sovereign nation and that impose far less restrictions on foreign investment than the various foreign investment restrictions China has always maintained, ever since the establishment of the PRC, including the 'open door' period in post-Mao China.

There is, however, one unintended consequence for China in imposing its trade 'sanctions' on Australia. For many years, China has challenged many Western countries in their assertion that China is not a market economy. Similarly, this question has been debated among academics (Zhou, Gao, & Bai, 2019). Considering China's centrally coordinated and implemented coercive practices towards many smaller economies, such a debate can now be seen as misleading and meaningless. If China does not distinguish state from the Party and the Party controls everything and every market process, there can be no market economy in China.[36]

5. Conclusion

The jewel in the crown, or not, clearly, WTO dispute settlement mechanism, just like any international law – multilateral, regional or bilateral – could not resolve a fundamental problem in international relationship and international law: 'international law is powerful against the powerless, and powerless against the powerful' (Chellaney, 2019). Superpowers do not have a good track record in accepting international dispute resolution (Chellaney, 2019), except, to a certain extent, in commercial arbitration and, until quite recently, the WTO mechanism. However, for an emerging power it must be remembered that this is an exercise in building trust and gaining confidence on a global stage.

The fact that the WTO dispute resolution processes are imperfect does not necessarily mean that international law is useless and meaningless. Indeed, the law of the jungle has always been part of the so-called rule-based international order and international law continues to develop, with international communities being fully aware of fundamental problems of power imbalances in international law. Perhaps the international community should aim for a less than perfect option, one where international law will resolve most

Foreign Legislation and Other Measures in January 2021. None is, however, relevant to the present Australia-China disputes.

36 Not surprisingly, China has now withdrawn its WTO case to determine whether it should be granted the market economy status.

disputes among most members most of the time and, ideally, at the least cost with an optimum outcome for disputants.[37]

The WTO dispute settlement mechanism had worked reasonably well before the recent AB crisis and the rise of economies with entirely different political systems. Put simply, the WTO dispute settlement mechanism was established on the basis and presumption of a liberal economic system and a bona fide compliance, by WTO members, with prior agreed rules. Such a presumption is clearly unrealistic and does not reflect our real world. The WTO as a dynamic system must develop with time and address emerging issues. Indeed, even during the GATT period, the dispute settlement mechanism was facing challenges because the GATT system failed in its development to reflect 'the need to evolve the terms of the bargain itself in light of changed circumstance' (Trebilcock, Howse, & Eliason, 2012: 177). In other words, the future and the fate of the WTO dispute settlement mechanism depends on the responses of the WTO system as a dynamic system to new and emerging issues, including the rise of non-market economies; any attempt at reforming the dispute settlement mechanism, such as AB, can only be a temporary solution. Increasingly, the artificial division of the WTO functions into three of its core functions (Ellard, 2022) – negotiation, monitoring and dispute settlement – has now become clearly unrealistic; the effectiveness of each of the core functions clearly depends on the development of the WTO as a whole dynamic system that responds to changing and changed circumstances.

At the practical level, the solution to trading power imbalances lies in finding dispute resolution mechanisms through which the powerful, just as any international player, can be held accountable by international law.

References

Bahri, Amrita (2019), 'Appellate body held hostage': Is judicial activism at fair trial?' 53 *Journal of World Trade* 293.

Baweja, Sahajveer (2020), 'WTO's "crown jewel" under existential crisis: Problem explained', *Modern Diplomacy*, 29 May, available at https://moderndiplomacy.eu/2020/05/29/wtos-crown-jewel-under-existential-crisis-problem-explained/ (last accessed 18/10/21).

37 We are here, of course, paraphrasing the former Chief Justice of the US, Warren Burger, who once said, '[t]he obligation of our profession is . . . to serve as healers of human conflict. To fulfil our traditional obligation means that we should provide mechanisms that can produce an acceptable result in the shortest possible time, with the least possible expense and with minimum of stress on the participants. This is what justice all about' (Burger, 1982: 274).

Blumenthal, Dan (2018), 'Economic coercion as a tool in China's grand strategy', 24 July 2018, available at www.foreign.senate.gov/imo/media/doc/072418_Blu menthal_Testimony.pdf (last accessed 5/4/22).

Bown, Chad (2009), *Self-Enforcing Trade: Developing Countries and WTO Dispute Settlement* (Washington, DC: Brookings Institution Press).

Burger, Warren (1982), 'Isn't there a better way', 68 *ABA Journal* 274.

Busch, Marc L. & Reinhard, Eric (2003), 'The evolution of GATT/WTO dispute settlement', available at https://georgetown.app.box.com/s/h0cf0gjf174crj3cdiv dgudzxbsofemf (last accessed 16/2/22).

Charnovitz, Steve (2017), 'How to save the WTO dispute settlement from the trump administration', International Economic Law and Policy Blog, available at https://worldtradelaw.typepad.com/ielpblog/2017/11/how-to-save-wto-dispute-settlement-from-the-trump-administration.html (last accessed 16/6/22).

Chellaney, Brahma (2019), 'The illusion of a rules-based global order', *Project Syndicate*, 20 December 2019, available at www.project-syndicate.org/com mentary/china-makes-mockery-of-international-law-by-brahma-chellaney-2019–12?from=groupmessage&isappinstalled=0 (last accessed 21/12/1).

Chen, Duanjie (2019), 'Countering coercion China's economic: No fear but resolve, no illusion but diversification', Canadian Public Policy, September 2019, available at https://macdonaldlaurier.ca/files/pdf/20190827_China_Economic_Coer cion_Chen_PAPER_FWeb.pdf (last accessed 5/4/22).

Chen, Jianfu (2016), 'Out of the shadows and back to the future: CPC and law in China', 24 (2) *Asia Pacific Law Review* 176.

Chen, Jianfu (2020), 'Chinese law & legal reform: Where to from here', 50 (1) *HKLJ* 243.

Chen, J. & Walker, G. (eds.) (2004), *Balancing Act: Law, Policy and Politics in Globalisation and Global Trade* (Sydney: Federation Press).

Choudhury, Saheli Roy (2020), 'Here's a list of the Australian exports hit by restrictions in China', 17 December, available at www.cnbc.com/2020/12/18/australia-china-trade-disputes-in-2020.html (last accessed 28/3/22).

Coates, Benjamin (2019), 'A century of sanctions', Ohio State University, December, available at https://origins.osu.edu/article/economic-sanctions-history-trump-global?language_content_entity=en (last accessed 29/3/22).

Communication (2018a), 'Communication from the European Unio', China, Canada, India, Norway, New Zealand, Switzerland, Australia, Republic of Korea, Iceland, Singapore and Mexico to the General Council, available at http://trade.ec.europa.eu/doclib/docs/2018/november/tradoc_157514.pdf (last accessed 26/3/22)

Communications (2018b), 'Communication from the European union', China and India to the General Council, available at http://trade.ec.europa.eu/doclib/docs/2018/november/tradoc_157514.pdf (last accessed 26/3/22).

Creamer, Cosette D. (2019), 'Can international trade law recover? From the WTO's crown jewel to its crown of thorns', 113 *AJIL* 51.

Crossley, Gabriel & Needham Kirsty (2021), 'China suspends economic dialogue with Australia as relations curdle', *Reuter*, 6 May, available at www.reuters.com/world/china-suspend-economic-dialogue-mechanism-with-australia-2021-05-06/ (last accessed 6/4/22).

Deudney, Daniel & Meiser, Jeffery (2012), 'American exceptionalism', in Michael Cox & Doug Stokes (eds.), *US Foreign Policy*, 2nd edition (Oxford: Oxford University Press).

DFAT (undated), 'China country brief: Bilateral relations', Department of Foreign Affairs and Trade, Australian Government, available at www.dfat.gov.au/geo/china/china-country-brief#:~:text=China%20is%20Australia%27s%20largest%20two,per%20cent%20during%20this%20period (last accessed 4/4/22).

Dube, Rohit (2022), 'Huawei's role in Chinese espionage and information operations', *Pre-Print*, 27 March, available at www.researchgate.net/publication/359582343_Huawei%27s_role_in_Chinese_espionage_and_information_operations (last accessed 4/4/22).

Ellard, A. (2022), 'DDG Ellard: WTO is essential to the rules-based international order', *WTO News*, 31 March 2022, available at www.wto.org/english/news_e/news22_e/ddgae_31mar22_e.htm (last accessed 5/4/22).

Financial Times (2022), 'Australia offers timely lessons in resisting Chinese trade coercion updates & news', *Financial Times*, 9 February, available at www.ft.com/content/fcb3590b-e468-4b88-9fba-217f54bd49d8 (last accessed 10/2/22).

Gao, Henry (2021), 'Finding a rule-based solution to the appellate body crisis: Looking beyond the multiparty interim appeal arbitration arrangement', 24 (3) *Journal of International Economic Law* 534.

Haass, Richard (1998), *Economic Sanctions and American Diplomacy* (Washington, DC: Council on Foreign Relations Press).

Hanania, Richard (2020), 'Ineffective, immoral, politically convenient: America's overreliance on economic sanctions and what to do about It', Cato Institute Policy Analysis No 884, 18 February 2020.

Hanson, Fergus, Currey, Emilia & Beattie, Tracy (2020), *The Chinese Communist Party's Coercive Diplomacy* (The Australian Strategic Policy Institute), available at www.aspi.org.au/report/chinese-communist-partys-coercive-diplomacy (last accessed 4/4/22).

Harris, Mark (2014), 'Beyond Doha: Clarifying the role of the WTO in determining trade-environment disputes', in Chen & Walker (2004).

Hart, Nina M. & Murrill, Brandon J. (2021), *The World Trade Organization's (WTO's) Appellate Body: Key Disputes and Controversies* Washington: Congressional Research Service.

Hartcher, Peter (2021), 'Huawei? No way! Why Australia banned the world's biggest telecoms firm', *The Sydney Morning Herald*, 21 May 2021, available at www.smh.com.au/national/huawei-no-way-why-australia-banned-the-world-s-biggest-telecoms-firm-20210503-p57oc9.html (last accessed 4/4/22).

Islam, M. Rafiqul (1993), 'GATT with emphasis on its dispute resolution system', in Wilde (ed.) (1993).

Jackson, John H. (1989), *The World Trading System: Law and Policy of International Economic Relations* (Cambridge, MA: The MIT Press).

Kearsley, Jonathan, Bagshaw, Eryk & Galloway, Anthony (2020), '"If you make China the enemy, China will be the enemy": Beijing's fresh threat to Australia', *The Sydney Morning Herald*, 18 November 2020, available at www.smh.com.

au/world/asia/if-you-make-china-the-enemy-china-will-be-the-enemy-beijing-s-fresh-threat-to-australia-20201118-p56fqs.html (last accessed 6/4/22).

Kohona, Palitha T. B. (1994), 'Dispute resolution under the word trade organisation', 28 (2) *Journal of World Trade* 23.

Lehne, Jens (2019), *Crisis at the WTO: Is the Blocking of Appointments to the WTO Appellate Body by the United States Legally Justified?* (Berlin/Bern: Carl Grossmann Publishers), available at https://crsreports.congress.gov/product/pdf/R/R46852 (last accessed 11/3/22).

Lester, Simon (2022), 'Ending the WTO dispute settlement crisis: Where to from here?' 2 March 2022, available at www.iisd.org/articles/united-states-must-propose-solutions-end-wto-dispute-settlement-crisis (last accessed 21/3/22).

Lester, Simon, Mercurio, Brian & Davies, Arwell (2018), *World Trade Law: Text, Materials and Commentary*, 3rd edition (Oxford/London/New York/New Dehli & Sydney: Hart).

Matsushita, Mitsuo, Schoenbaum, Thomas J., Mavroidis, Petros C. & Hahn, Michal (2015), *The World Trade Organisation: Law, Practice, and Policy* (Oxford: Oxford University Press).

Moore, Mike (2003), *A World Without Walls: Freedom, Development, Free Trade and Global Governance* (Cambridge, UK: Cambridge University Press).

Payne, Marise (Minister for Foreign Affairs and Trade, Australia) (2021), 'Address to Australia China business council', 5 August, available at www.foreignminister.gov.au/minister/marise-payne/speech/address-australia-china-business-council (last accessed 4/4/22).

Payosova, Tetyana, Hufbauer, Gary Clyde & Schott, Jeffrey J. (2018), 'The dispute settlement crisis in the world trade organization: Causes and cures', Policy Brief, Peterson Institute for International Economics, March 2018.

Pescatore, P. & Lowenfelf, A. F. (1992), *Handbook of GATT Dispute Settlement* (New York/Deventer: Kluwer Law and Taxation Publishers).

Petersmann Ernst-Ulrich (2018), 'The 2018 American and Chinese trade wars risk undermining the world trading system and constitutional democracies', EUI Working Paper Law 2018/17, available at https://cadmus.eui.eu/bitstream/handle/1814/59444/LAW_2018_17.pdf?sequence=1&isAllowed=y (last accessed 27/3/22).

Rathore, Aditya & Bajpai, Ashutosh (2020), 'The WTO appellate body crisis: How we got here and what lies ahead?" 14 April, available at www.jurist.org/commentary/2020/04/rathore-bajpai-wto-appellate-body-crisis/ (last accessed 21//22).

Robertson, Jordan & Tarabay, Jamie (2021), 'Chinese spies accused of using Huawei in secret Australia telecom hack', *Bloomberg*, 17 December, available at www.bloomberg.com/news/articles/2021-12-16/chinese-spies-accused-of-using-huawei-in-secret-australian-telecom-hack (last accessed 17/12/21).

Ryan, Mitch (2020), 'China-Australia clash: How it started and how it's going', 9 December, available at https://asia.nikkei.com/Politics/International-relations/China-Australia-clash-How-it-started-and-how-it-s-going (last accessed 4/4/22).

Sanger, David E. & Haberman, Maggie (2016), 'In Donald Trump's worldview, America comes first, and everyone Eles pays', *The New York Times*, 26 March.

Sheldon, Ian M. et al. (2018), 'Trade liberalization and constraints on moves to protectionism: Multilateralism vs. Regionalism', 100 *American Journal of Agricultural Economics* 1375.

Stewart, Terence P. (2018), 'The broken multilateral trade dispute system', Washington International Trade Association, 7 February, available at www.wita.org/blogs/the-broken-multilateral-trade-dispute-system/ (last accessed 27/3/22).

Tai, K. (2021), 'Ambassador Katherine Tai's remarks as prepared for delivery on the world trade organization', Geneva, October, available at https://ustr.gov/about-us/policy-offices/press-office/speeches-and-remarks/2021/october/ambassador-katherine-tais-remarks-prepared-delivery-world-trade-organization (last accessed 21/3/22).

Tan, Su-Lin (2020), 'What happened over the first year of the China-Australia trade dispute?' *South China Morning Post*, 28 October, available at www.scmp.com/economy/china-economy/article/3107228/china-australia-relations-what-has-happened-over-last-six (last accessed 4/4/22).

Timeline (2020), 'Timeline: Tension between China and Australia over commodities trade', available at www.reuters.com/article/us-australia-trade-china-commodities-tim-idUSKBN28L0D8 (last accessed 4/4/22).

Trebilcock, M. J., Howse, R. & Eliason, A. (2012), *The Regulation of International Trade*, 4th edition (London/New York: Routledge).

Uren, David (2020), 'Economic coercion: Boycotts and sanctions – preferred weapons of war', The Australian Strategic Policy Institute, October, available at www.aspi.org.au/report/economic-coercion-boycotts-and-sanctions-preferred-weapons-war (last accessed 5/4/22).

The USTR (2019), 'Trade policy agenda and 2018 annual report of the president of the United States on the trade agreements program', available at https://ustr.gov/sites/default/files/2019_Trade_Policy_Agenda_and_2018_Annual_Report.pdf (last accessed 5/5/22).

VanGrasstek, Craig (2013), *The History and Future of the World Trade Organization* (Geneva: World Trade Organization).

Vermulst, Edwin & Driessen, Bart (1995), 'An overview of the WTO dispute settlement system and its relationship with the Uruguay round agreements', 29 (2) *Journal of World Trade* 131.

Wang, Z. & Chen, J. (2019), *Dispute Resolution in the People's Republic of China* (Leiden/Boston: Brill Nijhoff).

Wiśniewski, R. (2021), 'Economic sanctions as a tool of China's hybrid strategies', *Polish Political Science Yearbook*, available at https://heinonline.org/HOL/LandingPage?handle=hein.journals/ppsy50&div=42&id=&page= (last accessed 5/4/22).

WTO (2018), 'Adjudicative bodies: Adding to or diminishing rights or obligations under the WTO agreement', WT/GC/W/754/Rev.2, December 2018, available at https://docs.wto.org/dol2fe/Pages/SS/directdoc.aspx?filename=q:/WT/GC/W754R2.pdf&Open=True (last accessed 26/3/21).

Wu, Mark (2016), 'The "China Inc" challenge to global trade governance', *Harvard International Law Journal* 261.

Zhang, Ketian (2018), 'Calculating bully – explaining Chinese coercion', PhD thesis, MIT, 2018, available at https://dspace.mit.edu/handle/1721.1/122472 (last accessed 5/4/22).

Zhou, W. & Laurenceson, J. (2022), 'Demystifying Australia-China trade tensions', 56 *Journal of World Trade* 51.

Zhou, W., Gao, H. & Bai, X. (2019), 'Building a market economy through WTO-inspired reform of state-owned enterprises in China', 68 *International and Comparative Law Quarterly* 977.

Conclusion

1. The Future of the International Economic Order

It is clear that since the conclusion of the Uruguay Round of negotiations that created the WTO, the WTO has failed to evolve with changing and changed circumstances and global economic cooperation has been in a state of constant struggle. Ironically, the Doha Round failed not because it did not try to respond to changed circumstances but, essentially, because its agenda was far too ambitious yet lacking specifics, far reaching yet lacking clear and direct links to trade. In other words, Doha wanted revolution but forgot that global trade regulation only works well in evolution. Added to this woe of the failed Doha round, has been the rapid development of regional agreements that divided the world in a time of increasing deglobalisation. But most critically, recent trade history is increasingly becoming a geopolitical race to hegemony rather than a period of accommodation, a period of conflict rather than cooperation, a time of rejection rather than reform. As such, our present time is described by some as the 'darkest era of the multilateral trading system' (Lee-Makiyama, 2021).

There is no doubt that major reforms of the multilateral international trading system are needed and, indeed, there are many reform proposals that have been made in the last many years, especially since the Doha Round was stalled after the Hong Kong meeting in 2015.[1] However, there is hardly any consensus among the international community as to how the multilateral trading system might be reformed.

Initial reform proposals seemed to focus on the scope of negotiations and many technical aspects of the WTO that need 'modernisation'. This

1 In relation to WTO reforms, there are many reform proposals from individual countries as well as groups of countries. For some major proposals, see EU, 2018; Joint Communiqué, 2018; Procedures, 2018); MOFCOM, 2019.

DOI: 10.4324/9781003275510-7

approach is most clearly reflected in the EU's Concept Paper: WTO Modernization (EU, 2018). The EU concept paper proposes that the WTO address the issue of market access, discrimination and regulatory barriers in all sectors, and the question of sustainability. It suggests the closer scrutiny of the use of industrial subsidies, trade-distortive subsidies, and the conduct of state-owned enterprises, as well as the creation of new rules to address issues such as forced technology transfer, market access barriers, discriminatory treatment of foreign investors and barriers to digital trade. The EU concept paper also opposes the broad exemptions enjoyed by developing countries and calls for flexibilities in the use of exemptions. It suggests that the multilateral negotiations should be supported but, if it is unattainable, plurilateral negotiations should be open, and new plurilateral agreements on the basis of MFN should be provided and their amendment procedure should be simplified. Fundamentally, the EU concept paper proposals are to broaden the scope of negotiation with the purpose of rebalancing the system and levelling the playing field.[2] Although, China was not named in the paper, the phrase 'rebalancing the system and levelling the playing field' is a sufficient reminder of this emerging power and its influence in the reform of the WTO. In this regard, the position of the Triliteral Partnership is critical,[3] which in fact always placed emphasis on levelling the playing field of international trade.

China declared its own position regarding the reform of the WTO in November 2018 and its suggestions for reform in May 2019 (Ministry of Commerce PRC (MOFCOM), 2019). China's position is summarised in its three principles for reform: the maintenance of the core values of the multilateral trade mechanism (no discrimination and open market), protecting the interests of the developing member countries, and maintaining the mechanism based on consensus between members. It further proposes five points of actions: maintaining the major channels of the multilateral trade mechanism, prioritising the key issues in relation to the operation of the WTO, enhancing fairness in trade between member countries in response to their contemporary needs, protecting the special and differential needs of

2 As a comprehensive proposal, it also addresses issues relation to transparency and the implementation, sanctions and dispute resolution.

3 The Trilateral Partnership (US, EU and Japan) is the successor of the old 'Quad' (US, EU, Japan and Canada). See Lee-Makiyama, 2021. Indeed, the partnership is named 'Trilateral Cooperation on Global Level Playing Field'. Its positions are expressed in its Joint Statement released after each of its meetings, which are contained on the website of the United States Trade Representative (https://ustr.gov).

developing member countries, and respecting the varied modes of development adopted by different member countries.

If all reform questions lead to China (Linscott, 2021), a uniform consensus among WTO members will be, clearly, hard to achieve. The earlier brief discussions suggest that the developed countries, such as the US, EU, Japan and Canada, actively seek the reform on substantive obligations, such as limiting the differential treatment of developing countries, focusing on the forced technology transfer, competition neutrality, punitive measures for non-compliance of notification requirements and so on. These measures, from the point of view of countries like China, were unfavourable to them. China sees these proposed reforms as *de facto* discrimination against its economy. China raised concern that these proposed measures could lead to the abuse of trade remedies and agriculture subsidies by developed countries (Liao, 2019: 43).

If it was hoped that the election of the Biden Presidency would ease the tension between China and the US and, hence, lead to some consensus on the reform of the multilateral trade system, it is increasingly clear that that was not the case. Not only has the Biden Administration so far maintained all the tariffs and measures imposed on China by the Trump Administration, it has also become clear that it now incorporates its security considerations into any trade negotiations. Thus, the recently issued Indo-Pacific Strategy (Indo Pacific Strategy, 2022) is clearly a part of the parties' security considerations and, indeed, the Indo-Pacific Economic Framework for Prosperity (IPEF) (Joint Statement, 2022) is no longer a traditional trade only framework. On the other hand, China also made it clear that it wants a new international governance mode based on its idea of a human community of shared destiny. Thus, as recently as May 2022, Chinese Foreign Minister Wang Yi, conducting an on-line meeting with Cambodian Deputy Prime Minister and Foreign Minister, stated that 'Facing various new global challenges, President Xi Jinping successively proposed the Global Development Initiative (GDI) and the Global Security Initiative (GSI). From the perspective of building a community with a shared future for mankind, he put forward a Chinese approach to establishing a global governance system with greater justice and equity, which has been widely supported and echoed by the international community, especially Asian countries' (Wang, 2022). Minister Wang Yi then declared that global governance is now ushering in an 'Asian Moment'. It seems that the two superpowers both want some kind of new international economic order, rather than reforming the existing one. In this context, the global community is facing a very serious ideological and value conflict and, hence, uncertainty and tension in international governance, including that in the multilateral trade regime.

2. A Dynamic System and its Means to Survival

The world trade regulatory system is a dynamic mechanism, composed of principally the GATT/WTO but supplemented by regional and bilateral trading agreements. However, the GATT/WTO system is different from most other international, regional and bilateral systems in that the requirement for change, development and evolution is inbuilt in the system. Such a system is meant to be stable, but not static, and it must evolve with changing and changed circumstances.

As a dynamic system, forces that propel the GATT/WTO evolution and development and maintain its stability are themselves evolving, as the world economic (but especially trading) powers change places and positions all the time. In the pre-WTO years, the GATT was both stable and dynamic and it worked and managed changes reasonably well. This is largely attributed to the existence of an economically unchallenged hegemon – the US as supported by its allies – as well as its narrow focus on trade issues. The WTO years have been very different. We saw the emergence of China and, to a less degree, India, Vietnam and many other emerging countries as major economic powers which are capable of changing the dynamic factors that propel the development of the global and regional trade and its regulatory development. As the existing hegemon's position is challenged, evolution and development in international trade inevitably take on a geopolitical flavour. At the same time, we have also witnessed tremendous and continuing expansion of regulatory scope by the trade regulatory system, that is the WTO. So far, the global system has clearly failed to cope with these dynamic changes. These forces represent those different interests, global, regional or national, but always impact on the interests of individual nations operating in the international trade arena.

GATT/WTO operates best when it deals with trade issues; and its records on 'trade-related' issues are mixed. It has proven mostly ineffective when it addresses politically charged issues, such as special treatment for developing countries or regional trade agreements. Based on GATT/WTO past performance, it is doubtful that it would achieve much in the area of 'social issues' – issues that are not trade in nature but having potential major impact on certain human rights (e.g., labour standards, environment protection, etc.) brought about by trade liberalisation – as highlighted during the Uruguay Round (1986–93) of the GATT/WTO negotiations.

Reflecting on recent events, it could be that the accidental separation of the UN and GATT/WTO might in fact have been one of the most fortuitous events in international trade regulation in that the separation allows politically charged issues to be addressed by the UN, leaving the GATT/WTO to address direct trade issues and narrowly selected but carefully considered trade-related issues. In other words, WTO, on the one hand, must respond to changing and changed international trading circumstances and, on the other hand, be selective and realistic as to its own capacity and limits in taking on new international issues. This necessarily applies to WTO rulemaking/rule-alteration and dispute settlement. A balance between the needs and aspirations of WTO members needs to be found and maintained, but such a balance must also be a result of considered decisions made. The stark reality is, the choice of balance will determine the fate and future of the global trade regulatory system which, in turn, will also gravely impact on regional and bilateral systems.

In short, this dynamic system of international trade regulation works well when a proper balance of interests between the parties to that system is found, but such a balance is constantly challenged by newly emerging issues and powers. A never-ending cycle of evolution is thus the natural movement of this dynamic yet stable system. As such, emerging powers need to be accommodated, through reform, not rejection. For these purposes, US, China and all '[t]hose seeking closer economic integration have a special responsibility to be strong advocates of global governance reforms' (Stiglitz, 2016). Even if the next phase of international economic collaboration is not about closer integration but deglobalisation, the global community needs to manage the process better than it managed globalisation (Stiglitz, 2022), as there are no other alternatives to collaboration when the countries in the world are already inter-dependent.

References

EU (2018), 'Concept paper: WTO modernization', September 2018, available at http://trade.ec.europa.eu/doclib/docs/2018/september/tradoc_157331.pdf (last accessed 10/5/22).

Indo Pacific Strategy (2022), 'Issued by the US Government in February 2022', A copy is available at www.whitehouse.gov/wp-content/uploads/2022/02/US-Indo-Pacific-Strategy.pdf (last accessed 16/6/22).

Joint Communiqué (2021), 'Joint communiqué of the Ottawa ministerial on WTO reform', Australia, Brazil, Canada, Chile, European Union, Japan, Kenya, Korea, Mexico, New Zealand, Norway, Singapore and Switzerland, available at www.wto.org/english/news_e/news18_e/dgra_26oct18_e.pdf (last accessed 14/5/22).

Joint Statement (2022), 'Joint statement on Indo-Pacific economic framework for prosperity', 23 May 2022, available at www.dfat.gov.au/news/media-release/launch-indo-pacific-economic-framework-prosperity-ipef-joint-statement (last accessed 24/5/22).

Lee-Makiyama, Hosuk (2021), 'A working party of three: The relevance of the trilateral cooperation on global level playing field', Policy Briefs, 2021/46, Global Governance Programme, EU-Asia Project, European University Institute, available at https://cadmus.eui.eu/bitstream/handle/1814/72860/QM-AX-21-046-EN-N.pdf?sequence=4&isAllowed=y (last accessed 12/5/22).

Liao, Fan (2019), 'WTO reform: Global agenda and China's position', 2 *International Economic Review* 32.

Linscott, Mark (2021), 'For WTO reform, most roads lead to China. But do the solutions lead away?' *The Atlantic Council*, 17 March 2021, available at www.atlanticcouncil.org/blogs/new-atlanticist/for-wto-reform-most-roads-lead-to-china-but-do-the-solutions-lead-away/ (last accessed 12/5/22).

MOFCOM, 2019, Suggestions on the Reform of the WTO by the Chinese Government (2019), available at http://images.mofcom.gov.cn/sms/201905/20190514094326062.pdf (last accessed 14/5/22).

Procedures (2018), 'Procedures to enhance transparency and strengthen notification requirements under WTO agreements', Communication from Argentina, Costa Rica, the European Union, Japan, and the United States, available at www.wto.org/english/news_e/news18_e/good_12nov18_e.htm (last accessed 14/5/22).

Stiglitz, Joseph E. (2016), 'The new geo-economics', *Project Syndicate*, 8 January, available at www.project-syndicate.org/commentary/hope-for-better-global-governance-by-joseph-e – stiglitz-2016–01?barrier=accesspaylog (last accessed 7/8/18).

Stiglitz, Joseph E. (2022), 'Getting deglobalization right', *Project Syndicate*, 31 May, available at www.project-syndicate.org/commentary/deglobalization-and-its-discontents-by-joseph-e-stiglitz-2022-05 (last accessed 7/6/22).

Wang, Yi (2022), 'Wang Yi holds virtual meeting with Cambodian deputy prime minister and foreign minister Prak Sokhonn', *Ministry of Foreign Affairs*, 8 May 2022, available at www.fmprc.gov.cn/mfa_eng/wjb_663304/wjbz_663308/activities_663312/202205/t20220509_10683416.html (last accessed 14/5/22).

Index

Note: Numbers in **bold** indicate a table.

For Product Safety Concerns and Information please contact our EU
representative GPSR@taylorandfrancis.com
Taylor & Francis Verlag GmbH, Kaufingerstraße 24, 80331 München, Germany

www.ingramcontent.com/pod-product-compliance
Ingram Content Group UK Ltd.
Pitfield, Milton Keynes, MK11 3LW, UK
UKHW022157190926
475702UK00003B/68
* 9 7 8 1 0 3 2 2 3 0 5 2 8 *